HOW TO GET INTO OXFORD AND CAMBRIDGE: BEATING THE BOFFINS

Geoff Moggridge,
Peter North,
Reg North

PGR Publishing,
Cambridge

First published 1998
by PGR Publishing
35 Christchurch Street
Cambridge, CB1 1HT
England

ISBN 0 9533186 0 5

Cover Design: Bernadette North

Photograph: Lindy Cahill

Printed by Coleraine Printing Company, BT52 2DZ.
Tel: 01265 54873

Vine House Distribution Ltd., Chailey, BN8 4DR.
Tel: 01825 723398

TABLE OF CONTENTS

FOREWORD

Each year 20,000 potential undergraduates apply to Oxbridge but only 6,000 are chosen. This book is a practical guide, giving step by step advice about how to manage Oxbridge entrance. It is invaluable reading for sixth formers considering applying and for the teachers who advise them. The authors are uniquely placed to write this book. They combine an insider's view of the admissions process with an intimate knowledge of the sixth form applicants' experiences.

Dr Geoff Moggridge M.A. (Cantab.) Ph.D. is a Lecturer at the University of Cambridge and has interviewed candidates for admission to King's College every year since 1992, where he is a Director of Studies and Tutor.

Dr Peter North M.A. (Cantab.) D.Phil. is a graduate of Cambridge and a senior researcher at the Institute for Terrestrial Ecology. He has authored numerous articles in the international scientific literature.

Dr Reg North B.A., D.Phil., PGCE is a Senior Lecturer in Education at the University of Ulster and is a governor of a large grammar school. He has had twenty long years of experience teaching in secondary education and has prepared many students for Oxbridge entrance.

The authors wish to help widen access to Oxbridge. The admissions procedure often seems obscure and intimidating to many prospective candidates, particularly those from schools unfamiliar with Oxbridge entrance. We aim to level the playing field by opening up the selection process, and making available the best advice on how to succeed to all those who read our book.

Our book takes you through the entire process from how to choose your college and fill in your application form to best effect, to succeeding in the selection tests and interviews themselves. We include and analyse case studies from a range of subjects. These case studies are drawn from the experiences of recent applicants and provide the reader with detailed insights into the selection process. To help you prepare, we have included exercises that assist you to work out a personal strategy. We have also provided a wide range of typical interview questions that cover all subjects available.

We are deeply indebted for the generosity of the many sixth form students, Oxbridge graduates, teachers and lecturers who have helped us through their contributions to the book and their assistance in its trials. We hope that this book is of help to you and wish you success.

INTRODUCTION

Are you thinking of applying to either Oxford or Cambridge University - commonly called Oxbridge? We hope that this book will help you to succeed with your application. We will do our best to prepare you for this journey and point out the many potholes and quicksands. However, we know that it is you alone who are the traveller, so we have designed our guide to help you successfully negotiate the selection process. Our guide provides a do-it-yourself manual that will assist you in developing your own style and finding your personal pathway to success with the Oxbridge selection process.

How do we propose to set about this task? Firstly, we will provide you with the vital information you need or, in some instances, tell you where it can be found. Secondly, we will cover in a structured way all the aspects of the Oxbridge undergraduate selection process. This coverage will introduce you to a number of people who have recently made an Oxbridge application; some were successful, others were not. You will find their experiences of the process helpful in many ways. They will offer you a surrogate experience - a bit like being there yourself. Thirdly, throughout the guide you will be set a number of tasks to complete. These tasks will both help you build up a systematic personal strategy and give you an *aide memoire* that you can thumb through during your time at Oxford or

Cambridge. This book should become your personal possession in which your own thoughts and feelings can be expressed.

'*How to get into Oxford and Cambridge: Beating the Boffins*', does not replace the university and college prospectuses. These are vital reading and the main source of information about colleges, subjects and procedures. We have not replicated information that can be easily obtained from these official sources, and neither do we attempt to promote Oxbridge. Instead, '*Beating the Boffins*' helps you work out your strategies and equips you for the selection process. It should, however, be read alongside the official sources of information.

In putting together this guide we have collected the detailed accounts of many sixth-formers who have recently encountered the selection process. Their fresh views and comments are rich in sensitivity to the difficulties that you may encounter and we owe a great debt of gratitude to these students. Evidence was also gathered from the two universities, some of which is in the public domain. In addition we have an insider's view of the process from the university's perspective, as one of the authors has for many years interviewed and selected Oxbridge applicants. His experience of finding numerous good candidates failing to do themselves justice owing to a lack of preparation and understanding of the system has prompted him to co-author this book.

The admissions process is carried out by individual colleges and contains a number of elements, which we have used to structure this guide in a straightforward and logical fashion. We assist you in your consideration of the essential factors in your choice of college, and give a practical guide to completing the application form, the final element of the selection process that is entirely within your control. You are then taken through the selection process, highlighting critical aspects that you can seek to influence. The next two chapters take you inside the interview process proper by dealing with the personal interview and the crucial technical interview. In these chapters you will find a wide range of people of your age talking about their experiences of the Oxbridge selection process and a range of typical interview questions.

At times you may think the journey will be too tough. Our strong advice is to try it. The experience that it will provide will most likely be rewarding. The vast majority of the applicants - both successful and unsuccessful - with whom we spoke during the course of producing your guide, said they were glad that they had gone through the process, finding it both interesting and beneficial. Also, to state the obvious, if you're not in you can't win. In general, if you have A or A* grades in at least 50% of your GCSEs and are projected by your school to achieve at least AAB in your A-levels, then you should consider yourself a serious candidate for Oxbridge. Each year, many students enter Oxbridge who did not believe that they had a chance of success. In this respect, Pat's response was fairly typical:

> *The thing was I didn't really expect to get in when I arrived. And from my interviews I thought that I had confirmed it. I thought it must be a mistake when I got the offer. But then I began thinking back over the interviews and began to realise that maybe I'd said some good things too.*

If you have been one of the 6,000 selected from a field of 20,000, then you are most certainly worthy of your place and have the ability to excel in the Oxbridge environment: avoid being trapped by the so-called 'impostor syndrome'. A great many more, who either do not apply or are not selected, are also capable of doing well at Oxbridge. Our aim is to open up the workings of the selection system in order to remove misplaced feelings of 'unworthiness' and, most importantly, to maximise your chances of success.

OXBRIDGE ENTRANCE – AN OVERVIEW

Oxford and Cambridge Universities have evolved a unique entrance procedure that has accumulated a quirkiness and mythology of its own. While you do not have to understand the history and rationale behind this, there are certain essential procedures you should know about. In this chapter we clear the ground by summarising all the important points of which you must be aware and direct you to essential official sources of information.

The Oxbridge system

The academic life of the universities revolves primarily around faculties and departments, as in all other universities. These university-wide bodies determine all lectures, exams and course structures. However, all students, and almost all teaching staff, are additionally members of a college and this acts as far more than just a hall of residence. There are 31 colleges in Cambridge and 30 colleges plus five private halls in Oxford. Each college provides a Director of Studies whose responsibility it is to monitor and enhance the intellectual progress of students in their subject and to organise small group supervisions (usually one to three students to one tutor). These supervisions are what make the Oxbridge system of teaching unique in Britain; they are usually carried out by members of the college, and it is in this way that colleges contribute to the academic progress of their students.

Colleges are entirely responsible for the selection process - if and only if admitted by a college do you become a member of the university. The university sets quotas for the total number of places, the arts-science split and numbers for a few subjects for each college. Beyond this the colleges are entirely autonomous, although in practice they tend to admit numbers to each subject much as they did in previous years.

Oxford and Cambridge do differ in several important ways. At Oxford colleges the same tutor is usually responsible for both academic progress and pastoral care; at Cambridge the roles are usually separated. Oxford has historically had a particular reputation for Politics, Philosophy and Economics; Cambridge for Physics and Mathematics. The 'Tripos' degree structure at Cambridge makes it easier to progressively specialise or to change subject than at Oxford. Nevertheless, the similarities between the two institutions greatly outweigh the differences; your choice should essentially be one of personal preference and where you feel your subject is taught and structured in a style that most suits you. You cannot apply to both Oxford and Cambridge simultaneously, with the sole exception of organ scholarships.

How to apply

Applying to Oxbridge is straightforward. In the first instance contact the Oxford and/or Cambridge

Admissions Office and request a university prospectus. This will provide you with the starter-pack in which you can find the essential administrative details for making your application as well as the important addresses that you will need to find out further information. Both the Oxford and Cambridge University prospectuses are excellent and are also published on the Internet. When applying, you must specify your subject choice and college, although the latter can be allocated for you automatically if you so wish, through the 'Open Applications' procedure.

Choosing your subject

Choosing your subject should be your first and most important decision. Here you need professional advice from your subject and career teachers. Remember that many of the subjects taught at the universities are not available as A-level courses. You can obtain some information about subjects from the university and college prospectuses. For those applying to Cambridge, obtain a copy of Cambridge University Guide to Courses, where you will find the syllabus for each course. For both Oxford and Cambridge more detailed information on subjects and departments can also be found on each university's web page. Further information can be obtained from the subject departments within the university and college admissions tutors. Departments are the most under-used source of information, and the 'Boffins' will be happy to help with your enquiries, particularly during their Open Days. If possible visit both universities. Also check that your planned A-levels satisfy any course requirements. Even after advice and personal research you may still feel uncommitted to any particular subject or profession. Don't worry – this is quite normal. After all, in many instances, you will have studied only three subjects at A-level and have limited experience. For the undecided, the flexibility offered by the Cambridge Tripos may appeal.

The admissions process

The universities assert that they are selecting on the basis of academic potential. To assess this, colleges have a large amount of information available when they make their selection of candidates. They will always have your application form, your UCAS form and your school report. Included in these are your GCSE (or equivalent) exam results and predictions from your school of your A-level grades. In many subjects at many colleges (note that even within a single subject there is no standard procedure), samples of your schoolwork assessed by your teachers will also be requested in the form of essays, practical write-ups and so on. These will be assessed for quality and may also be used as a basis for discussion at interview. Additionally, written or oral tests are often set on the interview day, which can make a significant contribution to the admissions process. Finally there are interviews. Each candidate is interviewed at least once and will usually be seen by at least two interviewers. The number of interviews given to each candidate is usually between one and three and the format also varies widely, depending on both subject and college.

The colleges take all these pieces of information very seriously. However, almost all candidates have a good set of GCSEs, a strong school recommendation, and a prediction of at least AAB grades at A-level, so it is difficult to distinguish between candidates on this basis. This leaves the assessed written work and the interviews and these are the major criteria on which you will be judged, greater weight usually going to the interviews.

It may seem strange and rather unfair that the principal assessment criterion is effectively an oral examination, whilst most schoolwork is based around written exercises. Oxbridge used to run its own entrance examinations, but this was deemed to favour candidates from independent schools, which often used to provide special preparation classes for this exam. Thus there are few options left to Oxbridge for selection other than by interview.

Conditional offers

Successful candidates will be made a conditional offer, requiring certain A-level grades. Expect the conditional offer to be at least AAB, usually AAA and occasionally AAAA. Equivalent exams are used for overseas or Scottish candidates. Occasionally, the conditional offer may be the minimum possible of EE. These are called 'Matriculation Offers', and some colleges may make up to one third of their offers in this form. However, there is an unwritten expectation that the student will still attempt to excel at A-levels. If you are applying after taking your A-levels and meet the matriculation requirements, you will be made an unconditional offer.

At Cambridge, in addition to A-levels, many colleges use STEP (Sixth Term Examination Papers) and/or S (Scholarship)-levels, while Oxford rely instead on their own written tests given during the interview period. Oxford is considering adding STEP to supplement their conditional offers. STEP papers are set by the University of Cambridge Local Examinations Syndicate, and are taken immediately following A-level examinations at the beginning of July. The material examined is intended to be covered by your 'A' level syllabus. However, the style of questions is very different. They are typically more open-ended, requiring more discussion and speculation. More emphasis is given to testing thought than knowledge. Thus STEP and S-level papers are a harder version of A-level, but in principle can be done without extra lessons. In practice, however, most candidates who attempt the STEP or 'S' papers do have additional coaching from their schools, to get them used to the unfamiliar type of question encountered. Copies of the current syllabus, and papers from the last four years can be obtained from the University of Cambridge Local Examinations Syndicate. These should help you decide whether STEP is suitable for you. Even if you are not considering taking STEP, it is worth looking through past papers in your subjects, to give you an idea of the style and level of question you might face in an interview or test. The prospectuses clearly list which colleges require these exams, and in which subjects. This may be an important factor in deciding to which college you apply

The Pool

Each university operates a Pool. These are internal clearing-house systems and provide a mechanism for the redistribution of candidates between colleges. In cases where the first preference college feels that a candidate is suitable material but is unable to make an offer, the college will throw the application into the Pool. At Cambridge you choose second and third preference colleges, while at Oxford the Admissions Office allocates these choices to colleges that are under-subscribed in your subject. These colleges will have first and second option once your application is sent to the Pool. Approximately 25% of applicants are placed in the Pool, about 15% of whom subsequently receive an offer. It should be noted that the Pool system is imperfect and tends to rely more on personal relationships between directors of studies than on any rational criterion. There is a strong desire within colleges to make every effort to finish the tiresome admissions procedure before the Pool system even begins to operate. A college that picks out a candidate from the Pool may well request further interviews.

Critical dates

There are some critical dates of which you should be aware.

(a) Prospectuses are published for the coming academic year in March, and should be obtained directly from the universities and colleges.

(b Open Days are important events that you should try to attend. These are organised by individual colleges and by some subject departments. Open Days are organised from April to June each year. Most colleges have at least three Open Days, the dates of which are given in the university prospectus. To attend, you should make an early written application, as places are limited.

(c) The submission of your application form must be made by the 15th October. At Cambridge the application form is submitted directly to your first choice college, at Oxford it is submitted to the University Admissions Office. You must also submit your UCAS form to Cheltenham at the same time.

(d) Interviews usually take place in early December once the undergraduates have gone on Christmas vacation. At Cambridge, selection interviews usually take one day but at Oxford they can take up to three days.

(e)   Decision information is usually provided very quickly. In most cases you will be given the college's decision by early January. If you have been placed in the Pool, three outcomes are possible. You will be directly made an offer from another college, called for further interview by an interested college, usually during the first two weeks of January, or be told by your first choice college that no offer will be made. This final filtering is usually completed before the end of January.

Sources of information

It is vital that you obtain as much information as possible on Oxbridge. To assist you in beginning your search we have included the most imortant contact addresses in Appendix I.

CHOOSING YOUR COLLEGE

Oxford and Cambridge are unusual amongst British universities in having meaningful collegiate structures. The college you choose will become your home for three years, and will largely determine the people you meet and how you are taught. Remember that the college also chooses you. The act of choosing your college should couple personal or emotional feelings with a tactical rationale. These, often contradictory, considerations should each play their part in your choice. You may need to resolve the tension between applying to a college that offers an appealing environment and one where you have a greater chance of being selected.

One of the problems is that the choice is made within your imagination. In advising you how to choose a college, we present you with a range of factors that need to be considered and also direct you to sources of statistical interest. Your quest should be to find the best fit of your own desires and ambitions to the anticipated opportunities that colleges offer.

It is important to realise that the transaction is two-way. During your life in college you will be contributing to its qualities. Indeed, one of the selection criteria employed by your college may well be your potential contribution to its community. Emmanuel College of Cambridge University nicely makes this point in its prospectus:

The character of a college is a composite of all the things mentioned in a prospectus, yet it is also much more than that. It is more dynamic. Its essence lies in the people within the college and their responses to their surroundings. The experience you will have .... depends both on those who have made their lives teaching and working in the college and on those who will share your time in the college as your contemporaries.

Beyond narrow academic considerations, colleges provide a high level of pastoral care and create the intellectual, sporting, social and artistic environments in which their students grow and flourish. In all these aspects colleges vary widely in character. It is not that one is better than another, rather that all are different and may suit your preferences differently.

Information sources

There is a considerable range of sources available to assist you in making your choice of college (see Appendix I for addresses). Paper-based sources include the university prospectus and college prospectuses. These can be obtained directly from each university's Admissions Office and the specific college. They are essential reading and will provide you with a good all-round understanding of admission procedures, subjects and a thumb-nail sketch of each college. These prospectuses should be read carefully and be seen as your detailed guide on regulations and procedures as well as your main sources for subject and college choice. Although accurate, these prospectuses do not tell you everything. After all, the university and the college are trying to attract you. Nevertheless, read them carefully, paying attention to specific emphases such as 'the College is particularly active in its encouragement of talented musicians' or 'College sports facilities are excellent... boasts highly successful soccer, rugby and hockey teams' (although beware, even Manchester United could slip into the First Division) or 'generous awards are available for those graduating with distinction in Law or Medicine to assist with their subsequent professional training' (this usually means that places in Law and Medicine will be highly competitive) or 'we are involved in a special initiative to increase the number of candidates from socially and educationally disadvantaged backgrounds' (this may mean you will receive some extra consideration, although you should be aware of the cosmetic nature of some such statements). Where you have specific interests you hope to pursue or take up, pay attention to tangible facts on facilities such as whether the college has a darkroom or modern squash courts.

The Students' Unions of Oxford and Cambridge each publish an Alternative Prospectus. These offer more information about the kinds of things not mentioned in the official prospectuses plus a "student's" view. This information includes some additional perspectives on the cultural and social life of colleges and departments.

Cambridge University also sells or rents a video which will provide you with some further reassuring information that will add to your growing sense of the flavour of Oxbridge.

Both Oxford and Cambridge Universities and their colleges also publish their prospectuses electronically on the Internet and may be accessed through the university's home page (Internet address is given in Appendix I). These are worth exploring. As you will find, colleges' web pages vary considerably in helpfulness. Some are excellent: user-friendly and packed with information. Some are very brief.

In addition to trying to assess colleges from virtual information, we recommend that you go there. Each college has Open Days that can help answer some of your questions. However, most Open Days are organised during vacation periods. This means that there will be only a few, if any, students around colleges. Try and pick a day during term time and just wander around the colleges to get a real feel of the place.

Practical considerations

Location

Both Oxford and Cambridge are university towns that have developed around the colleges. In the main the older colleges are located in the town centre. No college is more than a short bicycle ride from lecture halls, libraries, laboratories or sports fields. You may, however, feel that there are some advantages in your chosen college being located in the centre of the town or in having a river running through your back garden. Those colleges which are located in the town centre are well insulated from the outside noise and bustle by their usually pleasant gardens and high walls, although their attraction to tourists will, at times, bring the town to you.

Size

Colleges vary in size from 200 up to 650 undergraduates. The average size is about 320 undergraduates. In other words, there will be between 70 and 220 students in your year, depending on which college you choose. In terms of size, colleges represent the range of sixth forms from which most of you have come. But does size matter? That is for you to decide. In general, the larger colleges offer more choice in sporting and social events. You are more likely to find at least eleven people interested in playing soccer or a good-sized choir in a large college. Size may also affect the number and range of teaching fellows on offer, although all colleges support the main subjects and provide the same tutorial supervision

Bed & breakfast

Creature comforts may be important to you. In general, the food and dining arrangements in all colleges are very satisfactory, although the appeal of institutional cooking may well pall before the end of term. Most colleges raise a 'kitchen charge' at the beginning of term to encourage its members to dine in college. The resultant low cost meals have particular attractions towards the end of term when the grant or, more likely, the student loan is nearly exhausted. Some colleges still have what is referred to as formal hall where gowns are worn to dinner and a Latin grace is said. This, coupled with a high table, may appeal to you.

There is a considerable variation between colleges in the living accommodation offered. Most offer accommodation in college for first and third year undergraduates. Usually, colleges provide rooms in town houses during the second year. Some college rooms, particularly in older colleges, are, to say the least, rather basic, although they may be spacious and atmospheric. Many of these colleges have modernised their accommodation (principally to facilitate the conference trade - this may result in your being ejected immediately term ends). A benefit of choosing one of the new colleges is that you are more likely to be housed in modern quarters.

If you consider these aspects important then you should peek around doors and through windows during your Open Day visit.

Studying your subject
Getting a good degree is important. Each year at Oxford and Cambridge, an academic league table of colleges is published. This table ranks colleges in terms of the quality of the degrees obtained by students. There are large fluctuations from year to year, although some colleges manage to feature

regularly in the top ten. Many scholars are unimpressed with these tables. Unless you are sure that your college is consistently in the top quartile of the table, it would be unwise to cite it a reason for choosing your college. The tables are, however, possibly an indicator of the competitive intensity of the academic environment.

One of the factors that may well influence your choice is the academic support from within your college. You will note that each college prospectus lists its Tutorial Fellows or Teaching Officers and their subjects. Our advice is to take account of this list when selecting your college and ensure that the subject you wish to study is included. At Oxford this aspect is made clearer by the way the prospectus groups its colleges in terms of subjects offered or not offered

There are also advantages in being in a college that boasts several teaching fellows for your subject, as this is an indicator that there will be a number of contemporaries studying your subject. Although an advantage of college life is that you will have the opportunity to meet people studying a wide range of subjects, it is also very desirable to have colleagues in your subject.

Wealth and scholarships
Colleges vary considerably in the financial assets they have acquired over the centuries. We are not suggesting that you necessarily carry out a wealth check before choosing but some colleges are particularly generous in the way they award

scholarships and bursaries. You may feel that you might qualify for one of these and that it should be an element in your college decision-making process. We know of one, admittedly very wealthy college, which claims to have given away more money to support student bursaries, research and specific trusts than it spends on running the college.

Emotional reasons

Many of the Oxbridge colleges have been in existence for centuries and may claim luminaries, both living and dead, whom you may have come across in your studies or who were major figures in world events. Many colleges are also architecturally spectacular and have splendid gardens and scenic settings. These historical and aesthetic features may well create for you a unique atmosphere that offers strong personal attractions that will add to your motivation to study at a particular college.

Similarly, each college will have created its own ethos, reflecting its individual culture. This will be reflected by such things as institutional links, relationships between senior and junior members, artistic and sporting endeavours, social mix of students, gender balance etc. These factors will play their part in forming the world in which you will live for at least three years and should be considered when choosing your future college.

Tactical considerations

You will probably be eager to maximise your chances of being successful in the Oxbridge lottery and it is worth noting that colleges differ significantly in those vital statistics that may affect your chances of being selected. You will find some statistical data in each university prospectus and in some of the college prospectuses. You may find that Oxford University's prospectus is more helpful than Cambridge's in presenting a statistical picture. It offers more detail and includes all subjects. Cambridge, on the other hand, offers an easy to read colour chart but only for main Tripos subjects.

The most influential of these college statistics is **the ratio of applications to places**. Colleges vary dramatically in the numbers of applications they receive and the number of places they have available for particular subjects. For example, using the 1995-1997 average ratio of applications to places to read History at Oxford, there was a variation between colleges from 2:1 to 4:1. At Cambridge, where the public presentation of this kind of data is less detailed, there are similarly wide variations in the applications to places ratio. For example, using the 1995-1997 average for Medicine, the average over all colleges was 4.5:1, yet this varied between approximately 3:1 and 12:1. In other words, there would have been a staggering difference of a factor of four in the chances of being selected for Medicine depending upon which college was applied to, if all other factors had been equal.

The result of this is that your choice of college is significant in your chances of getting a place at the university.

You may feel this kind of statistical information is useful when making your final choice of college. However, caution is needed. All is not straightforward here: as the often cited quotation of Benjamin Disraeli points out *"There are three kinds of lies: lies, damned lies and statistics"*. If you are going to use published statistical information there are some health warnings you should know about.

Surprisingly, there has been stubborn stability in the ratio of applicants to places for most subjects within each college over the last decade. The larger subjects show a variation of about ±10%. For smaller subjects this is inevitably much greater. However, past performance is no guarantee of the future. Any number of things could change the pattern of applications such as a TV series or even this book.

These raw statistics also do not take account of candidates allocated through the Open Allocation procedure or the Pool. The Open Application procedure accounts for about 7% of applicants, who will be allocated to the least popular colleges in their subject. Similarly, Pooled candidates may be picked-up by the under-subscribed colleges. As you can imagine, these two groups can considerably change the balance of applications for subjects within a college, making it harder to make an effective tactical choice.

A further piece of statistical information is that Cambridge colleges differ in the number of offers they make, from 1.1 offers per place to 1.8 per place. This factor does not apply to Oxford, where all colleges use approximately the same ratio. Colleges which only make on average 1.1 offers for each place (i.e. eleven offers for ten places), will set 'realistic' A-level requirements and will be more flexible if you fail to meet these requirements. Be aware that this inevitably means a greater emphasis on the interview process. Those colleges which make 1.8 offers per place will set higher requirements for A-levels (and possibly also S-levels or STEP papers), thereby allowing the public examination system to carry out the final selection.

Although not listed in the current prospectus, the 1998 picture at Cambridge was as follows:

Colleges making up to 1.3 offers for each place: Christ's, Corpus Christi, Downing, Girton, Gonville & Caius, Jesus, Kings, New Hall, Newnham, Pembroke, Peterhouse, Robinson, Sidney Sussex, Trinity Hall.

Colleges making between 1.3 to 1.8 offers for each place: Churchill, Clare, Emmanuel, Fitzwilliam, Magdalene, Queens', St. John's, Selwyn, St. Catharine's, Trinity.

In addition to differences in the ratios of applications to offers, and in offers to places, colleges also differ in the **ratio of independent school to maintained (state) school** applications.

From a tactical point of view, we would not encourage use of this ratio. This is because generally the ratio of independent to maintained school undergraduates accepted appears to roughly match the same ratio of applications for each college. This information is not always easily accessible, although those colleges with a high proportion of maintained school undergraduates tend to make it a public virtue. Those colleges with low maintained school numbers have tended to attract the attention of the national press recently. The differences between colleges in the independent : maintained school ratio are large, varying from 1:5 to 3:1. Overall, both Oxford and Cambridge show a roughly even split. It is most unlikely that any college interviewer will consciously bias his or her judgements because of an applicant's background. In general, however, those colleges which have high numbers of maintained school undergraduates are also those which are most heavily over-subscribed.

Open applications
Consideration of using an Open Application should be on your tactical agenda. Currently about 7% of candidates use an Open Application. In tactical terms, the value of the Open Application is that the central admissions' computer selects your three colleges based upon an analysis of applications received by the colleges. In practice this means that your application will first be sent to the college with the lowest numbers applying for your subject. Once allocated to your college, you will be treated in the same way as other applicants who made the college their preferred option.

The clear advantage offered by the Open Application with respect to competition is not without its downside. For example, you may be allocated to an unpopular college, although many excellent colleges have shortages in applications for some subjects. If you are female there is a good chance that this system will place you in an all-female college. You must remember that once placed by the central computer, it is not possible to change your allocation of college. Another disadvantage is that you will lose control over such important things as avoiding the requirement to do STEP papers and the freedom to choose a college that makes a high number of offers per place or *vice versa*.

How far you go down the path of tactical choice when selecting your college is your decision. Remember, though, that at some point you will probably be faced with the interview question: "Mr Robinson, would you tell me why you have chosen to come to this college to study Law?" or, "Miss Robinson, would you like to tell me why you used the Open Application route and what do you think of the choice of college that has been made for you?"

Exercise 1 - Choosing your college

You might find it helpful to use the following framework when choosing your college. We suggest that you first select your college from the prospectuses without considering tactical factors. Once your provisional first choice of college is made, only then explore the statistical aspects that may modify your choice. These factors considered, we suggest that, for Cambridge only, you then select your second and third preference colleges. As your application will be forwarded to these colleges in turn, if you are not selected by your first choice college, it may be worthwhile fully utilising tactical factors when choosing second and third preference colleges.

Part 1 - Finding out what is important to you.
To assist in finding out what is important to you we suggest you complete the following table by entering a score between 1 and 5 for each question using the scale:

1= unimportant; 2= quite important; 3= important;
4= very important; 5= essential

    Practical
        location
        size
        comfort
        numbers studying your subject
        study facilities
        scholarships

    Emotional
        tradition
        architecture
        aesthetics
        formality
        social mix
        gender balance
        sport
        arts

Part 2 - **Provisional choice of college**

At this point, based upon your knowledge of what is important to you and using the information you have collected, make a provisional choice of first preference college. Score your college according to the criteria above.

Part 3 - **Checking out the statistics**

Once this provisional choice has been made we suggest you check out the college's vital selection statistics using the following check-list (note that (b) & (c) do not apply to Oxford):

(a)　Ratio of Applications to Offers for your subject
　　　High　　　Average　　　Low
　　　University Average_____

(b)　Ratio of Offers to places
　　　High　　　Average　　　Low

(c)　Step or 'S' level examination required
　　　Yes　　　No　　　　　N/A

Part 4 - Reconsidering your choice
In the light of the statistical data do you wish to change your first choice?

Part 5 - Making your choice
We suggest that you now try and select your colleges. Note that at Oxford the computer will select your 2nd and 3rd preference colleges.

1st Choice :

2nd Choice:

3rd Choice :

Now write two paragraphs that you could use to answer the questions "Why have you chosen Oxford/Cambridge to study ....?" and "Why did you choose .... College?"

University and Subject

College

Part 6 - Open applications

Would you mind not getting any of the above?
Would you prefer the university to choose for you?
If your answer is yes, write down the reasons for
this decision below:

THE APPLICATION FORM

There is a variety of application forms in both Oxford and Cambridge and you should consult the relevant prospectus to ensure that you get the correct one. However, the information required and the use to which it is put is very similar regardless of your category of application or the university to which you are applying.

The application form is often treated by applicants as merely a factual preliminary to the competitive stages of the admissions procedure. This is a severe mistake - your battle to impress starts when you put pen to paper. Your form is the first introduction the interviewer has to you - it is your opportunity to create a good impression. Even more importantly it is your opportunity to influence the interview process. Feed the interviewers with what you would wish to come up in the interview. On the whole interviewers are attempting to bring out the best in you and the form is your chance to help them. You must expect and be prepared to talk about what you have written on the form. You are almost inevitably on the defensive during interviews or tests. You will be nervous, questions will be coming thick and fast. It will be all you can do to keep going and you will have little chance to make rational tactical decisions or to manipulate proceedings. The application form is the one point at which you are fully in control - you have as much time as you like, and within the constraints of accuracy you can do what you like. It is not often appreciated how powerful this is and how important it is that you take full advantage of the opportunity. A well prepared application form will not get you in, but it should reduce your chances of walking away from the interview feeling that you have not given your best. To get the most out of the application form you must consider two things: what would you like to happen in the interview and what is the person reading the form making of each piece of information you supply. The combination of these two ideas must inform your decision of what to write.

Here we present a personal perspective written by one of the authors, who has to process many Cambridge application forms each year. There will be numerous differences of detail in the case of Oxford applicants, but the principles highlighted here will be fully applicable. The exercise at the end of the chapter should assist you to assemble the required information into any format.

Fill the application form out in black pen; follow the instructions exactly and make sure the result is accurate, easily read and neat. The best way to achieve this is to photocopy the blank form, fill it in completely and then copy the result onto the original. Under no circumstances make any spelling mistakes on the form; one or two crossings out are OK, but too many just make you look incompetent. Many candidates word-process their personal statements and glue them into the form - this is fine and often makes it easier to fit a lot of words neatly into the box. This should all sound like trivial advice, but it is astonishing how many sloppy forms are received - and however much one tries to avoid it, impressions do matter. Most importantly - take a photocopy of your completed form and keep it. You must read it before your interview. There is a long gap between filling in the form and being interviewed and it is vital that you know what they know about you. You may also have new things to add. After all nobody stands still.

In order to help you to think about the application form in a way which is helpful to you in making the most from it, I will consider each entry on the form separately. Some of the purely factual entries have been ignored. By far the most important aspect is your statement of personal and academic interests.

Personal details

The photograph. This is the cause of a huge amount of unnecessary worry. The purpose of the photograph is so that when your case is discussed after the interviews by all those involved in the decision, we can remember who you are. If you have interviewed fifty candidates in the preceding week, it can be immensely useful to have one's memory jogged by a picture to fill out sparse interview notes. In marginal cases (those we would take if we had enough places), and perhaps half of those we accept fall into this category, this post-interview discussion is critical and it is almost always an advantage if a living person is remembered rather than just the imprint of some dry notes. The only important thing about the photograph, therefore, is that it looks like you! Naturally, it is better to err on the flattering side, but this really is of very much secondary importance.

Name, initials, title, proposed subject. This is just factual information. It is repeated down the right hand side of the form so that it can be easily read either the right way up or in a filing cabinet. Make sure you get the letter as well as the spirit of your subject choice correct. For example if you wish to study Physics you need to write down Natural Sciences (Physical).

School. Again this is factual information beyond your control. However it is worth considering what interviewers may make of it. They may make a judgement (perhaps quite arbitrarily), based on your school type and reputation, as to the likely quality of your sixth form education. This can cut both ways; you can only make a judgement as to the likely impression and play to your strengths. If you go to Manchester Grammar and your school says you are one of its top two students of the year, this will be taken very seriously; however if you are applying to read Physics and display an inability to do calculus, a correspondingly dim view will be taken. If you are at Stony Bridge Comprehensive, high praise from your school will (maybe unfairly) be looked at more sceptically, but equally you could get more leeway on your technical skills (again, perhaps unfairly).

College. This is important both from a tactical and practical point of view; as discussed in the previous chapter.

Year of entry. Do you want a year off or not before coming to Oxford or Cambridge? You need to make your own decision here on whether to defer entry. A few subjects (Engineering for example) strongly advise a year off; others, such as Classics or Mathematics prefer immediate entry. If you are particularly young for your school year, it might marginally help to apply for deferred entry (sometimes Colleges will advise this anyway when making an offer). In terms of the chances of getting in, it should on average make no difference whether you apply for deferred entry or not. However it does change who it is you are competing with. If you defer, you no longer take away someone else's place directly by getting accepted. This can work either way - in a slack year you miss the opportunity of creeping in to make up the college's quota; in a strong year, you avoid the heat of direct competition. Most applicants choose not to defer.

Parental occupations. This is a bit like your school really. It creates an impression, which may be quite wrong. If your father is a Professor of History and your mother a French translator, a complete ignorance of the existence of Proust is unlikely to impress.

Qualifications

Academic qualifications. Nothing to be done about this, but be aware it will be looked at with some seriousness. Straight As does impress, one worries about too many Bs.

Additional subjects studied. These fall into two categories. First, those not involving examinations but enriching your sixth form education, such as a short course in Japanese or word processing. Second, those which are tested, but not by a GCSE, A-level or similar academic examination; these are often musical in nature. Some entries here do no harm to demonstrate how well-rounded an individual you are, but don't worry about leaving these boxes blank - don't invent things! Expect questions about overtones in vibrating strings if you have Grade 8 violin and are applying to do Physics or how planes stay up if you claim a glider pilot's license and want to be an Engineer. One of the things we like to feel we look for is candidates with an interest in areas relevant to their subject, but not directly involved in school syllabuses.

Work experience. If you have some put it down. Just make sure that if it is in any way relevant to your subject you can make the connections and talk sensibly about it.

Personal statements

Plans for time off. This applies only to those intending to, or in the process of, deferring. Put something interesting down, but be prepared to discuss this at interview.

Possible career. It is good to have some ideas even if they are very vague. Usually it is better if your ideas make some use of the subject you propose to study. It tends to be a put-off if you appear just to want the BA(Cantab) after your name so that you can get a highly paid City job.

Personal achievements and interests. This is the big one, your chance to show yourself as a lively, well rounded individual and to manipulate the subjects of the interview. It is also an opportunity to demonstrate your prose style; I would discourage a simple list of achievements. You are asked for both academic and non-academic interests and you should provide both. It can be identical to your UCAS statement, but on the whole I would advise against this, although it inevitably will be quite similar in content. There are two reasons for this. First you are aiming for something a bit different from the two forms. If you are applying to Oxford or Cambridge, you should be expecting to succeed fairly easily in your other applications - safety in these will suffice for UCAS. To get into Oxbridge you need to stand out from the crowd - this is your first opportunity to shine. You probably need to be a touch more daring. Secondly we have your UCAS form too - if you do something different, even if only slightly, it shows you have gone that extra mile. Some colleges will, in addition, ask you to fill in a questionnaire about your application and this may include your motivation for studying your chosen subject. The comments for the personal statement on the application form hold true.

The non-academic bit is basically your opportunity to set a background. What you need to be aiming for is to produce in the interviewer a warm glow of confidence that you are an interesting, social and competent human being. It doesn't much matter what you do, so long you show some enthusiasm for something, be it sport, music, the arts, botany or whatever. You don't have to have done anything desperately impressive - we understand that everyone has different opportunities, aspirations and abilities in the varied spheres of their lives. Put things down because you enjoy them and are interested in them not because you think you are good at them. Having said that, if you happen to be the West of Ireland chess champion don't hide the fact. The willingness and ability to compete will be respected - Oxbridge is a very competitive environment.

On the whole I would avoid things which make you look immature - I always find I have to brace myself not to be prejudiced against those who express a passion for role playing games or train spotting (and you'd be surprised how many there are). Equally avoid looking pompous or pretentious. No one expects you to have a view on 18th Century Montenegrin poetry - if you really do, then by all means say so, but don't invent an opinion just to impress. Try to avoid being excessively vague in your interests. The classic is to express an enjoyment of reading - well I hope so! Tell us that you like German crime thrillers, but make sure you have something to say about them. Something a little quirky can be good - I always enjoy seeing interests like beekeeping. At the same time, avoid appearing obsessive. This bit is all about balance. Whatever you put, make sure you can talk sensibly, and preferably interestingly about it (consider how dull a whole day's interviews could be). General interests are not going to get you in - only the technical stuff can do this - but they can get you off to a good start.

The most important part of the application form is putting down your academic interests. Here you have to be entirely cynical - you have to impress the interviewers and you have to feed them with the questions you want to be asked. Impressing need not involve showing a massive technical knowledge or vast list of readings - evidence of inquisitiveness and a desire to look beyond the school curriculum of your subject will suffice.

There are essentially two ways of feeding questions back to yourself. The first is to express interest in a particular subject area. The more specific the area, the easier it is for you to mug up on just before the interview (though beware of looking silly - no one is going to believe in your passionate interest in capacitor design, though they will buy a love of electronic circuitry). Don't just go for what is fashionable - every budding physicist seems to love astronomy at present (though surprisingly few know who Kepler was). If your real interest happens to be what is in the news that is fine, but if you are basically a generalist and are fairly arbitrarily choosing something (and you should do this - though don't choose something you really couldn't care less about), it is probably better to go for something more unusual. Most importantly don't choose something which you haven't got a cat's chance in hell of talking sensibly about. Discussing superstring theory with the Emeritus Professor of intergalactic maths can be a discomforting experience. The optimum would be to choose something pretty specific, just above the level of your syllabus and make a real effort to understand it in some depth shortly before the interview.

The second approach is to put down two or three books you have read. You don't have to have read them yet (though that might help in making a good selection), but you will have to read (or reread) them in the weeks preceding the interview. Once again it is critical that these books are neither too vague nor too difficult - Hawking, for example, is generally pretty useless. They should be things which take you a little further than (or at least out of) your A-levels and which you can understand. The interviewers need not have read the book but it helps if they have heard of it and know roughly what it's about. Stephen Jay Gould or Eatwell might be good examples. Most critically you need to understand the books and have some specific points you can pick up on and talk about in some depth.

I would suggest that you include both these strategies in your personal statement. They require preparation in the weeks before the interview and will backfire if this is not done properly. They are however your best opportunity to control the interview. If either specific subject-related reading or topics of particular interest are included, I always ask about them; I actively try to get into areas that interest the candidates and which they know something about and this is my best chance to do so. We can both know we are playing the game of feed-the-interviewer without it mattering; I am happy because it maximises my chances of getting the best out of you, you are happy because it makes the interview as predictable as possible. I am always amazed that 90% of the time I ask about these things, it turns out that the candidate has nothing to say on the subject - often they appear not even to have read the book they claimed to have done.

Sample personal statements

Below are two examples of what we consider might be good personal statements, followed by a description of the points that impress for the first, and an exercise for you to do for the second.

Natural Sciences (Physical)
My principal academic interest is physics. What I find particularly exciting about this subject is its ability to explain, from simple and often seemingly obvious axioms, both the everyday and the extraordinary in the world around us. For example, why does the pitch of an ambulance siren change as it whizzes past one? I enjoy reading around the subject to explore areas related to, but beyond the scope of the A-level course. I regularly read New

Scientist and also enjoy popular science books. I have recently read "Relativity" by Albert Einstein. It was fascinating to see how such a far reaching theory as Special Relativity could be built up from two simple ideas. Although I found the details of the latter parts of the book, involving General Relativity, beyond my technical ability, the insight into how the theory was developed further was nonetheless extremely stimulating.

Outside my academic studies I enjoy a diverse range of social and cultural pursuits. I play several sports with enthusiasm, if not great talent, competing for the school cross-country and second tennis teams. I have a love of the great outdoors and take great pleasure in hiking and camping in the wilder parts of the country. I listen to a wide range of music from jungle to classical, but my particular favourite is jazz, for which reason I have been learning the tenor saxophone for the past two years.

Description of good points
You have put two lines of enquiry at the disposal of the interviewer. These are subjects which show you have the initiative to think and inquire for yourself, but which you stand a good chance of being able to produce a lucid and accurate description of. If asked about the ambulance siren you can describe the principles of the Doppler effect for sound waves. For the interviewer there are several possible developments of this. One would be to consider the difference between the Doppler effect for sound and light. You need to make sure you can follow this

avenue - this is where you will really start to impress. Think about what you would ask if you were the interviewer and what connections you could make to related topics; don't, however assume that you will second guess any of the specific questions, although you might hope to predict a general line of enquiry. The fundamental importance of the speed of light in the Doppler effect can also link seamlessly into your second topic - Special Relativity. Be able to talk about this - it doesn't matter if you don't understand everything about it, just show some knowledge and interest. Although you have stated that the bit of the book on General Relativity was beyond you, it is highly likely that the interviewers will drag you into this area just to see how you cope, if they were impressed with your previous answers. It would do no harm to have up your sleeve a little more knowledge here than you cared to admit to, though it is certainly something no one can expect you to fully understand.

In terms of general interest, you have shown you get out, do things and enjoy life. You have also given plenty of opportunity for questions which you can talk easily about. It might even be of interest for the old crusties to discover what jungle is.

Social and Political Sciences

I have come to consider SPS principally as a result of aspects of my A-level courses. My politics course has developed my understanding of current politics and the history that has produced it. I find it particularly interesting to make connections between the theories covered in my schoolwork and real current political issues, such as the question of the future role of proportional representation in the British electoral system. My history syllabus provides a deeper insight into the origins of modern politics - the period covered is the mid nineteenth to the mid twentieth century. This reveals many interesting parallels with modern politics - for example, Gladstone's efforts to solve the Irish question have much to say to us about the current peace process.

My general interest in politics and the sociology which underpins it has also led me towards SPS. I read as widely as possible relevant literature - I am currently reading Alan Bullock's book "Hitler and Stalin: Parallel Lives", and often dip into the Economist. I am an active member of the Liberal Democrats; I have participated in campaigns for both local and national elections and regularly attend party meetings. I find that the Liberal Democrats' interest in constitutional reform sits particularly well with my academic interest in political theory. I am also a keen participant in the school debating club.

Beyond academic pursuits, I hill walk, play the violin and cultivate carnivorous plants.

Exercise 2

In the space provided below, fill in what you think the good points of this personal statement are and, if this were your personal statement, what preparations you would make for the interview to maximise these strengths. It should not matter what subject you are planning to study – you should be interested in structure and tactics here, rather than specific content. Our comments on this personal statement appear at the end of this chapter.

What does the interviewer do with your form?

This will vary somewhat from college to college and person to person, but the principles will be pretty similar. I will describe what I do.

The form itself is not taken into the interview. We have another form on which are printed your personal details. One section of this form is for my pre-interview notes. I put down the school's prediction of your A-level grades - if these are not straight As it is a worry. I also try to write down some assessment of your school reference (strong, weak, outstanding). I note your GCSE results (5A*s, 2As, 3Bs or whatever). If you have expressed an interest in anything to do with your subject I write this down, and I note any books you claim to have read. I will almost always ask about these points. I also try to put at least one general interest point down - I won't usually use this, but might start off with it if someone seems particularly nervous, or resort to it if they get totally bogged down, as a means of making a mild transition between technical topics. Recently, I have also taken to putting a star in my pre-interview notes for candidates who appear particularly strong from their application forms. This has proved a surprisingly reliable, though very far from infallible, guide to form; this indicates how significant the application form can be.

If you were asked to provide any written work or sit any tests, comments on this will also go into the pre-interview notes.

I usually read your form a few days before the interview and then have only these pre-interview notes to remind me of the salient points in the minutes before I talk to you. I have these notes available during the interview and the interview notes are added to the same form.

After all the interviews are finished we have a subject meeting with all interviewers present to decide whom to accept. We have all the application forms and our notes available at this point and in discussing marginal cases we always look again at the forms (this is where the photo is so useful). Thus the application form is both the first and last we see of you during the admissions procedure - use it well.

Notes on Exercise 2 - SPS personal statement

(a) Good points
Evidence of thinking about the nature of SPS and why to study this course.
Some specific points for the interviewer to raise:
- proportional representation from general interest
- Gladstone's Irish question from school work (both specific points with potential for broadening into interesting discussions)
- Bullock's book from general reading.
There is a nice potential connection between PR and interest in Lib Dem constitutional policy.

Interest is shown in subjects beyond the scope of school work and an ability to apply A-level ideas to everyday issues is demonstrated. There is evidence of relevant reading beyond the syllabus. Individuality and a life beyond school are clear.

A potential weak point, which might be explored in interview - does the applicant have a balanced academic approach? Is she prepared to show the same interest in the development of Marxist theory as she has shown in PR? Just something to think about.

(b) Preparation for interview
Think about and make notes on the issues mentioned: perhaps you have already written a school essay related to one of them. Think about how you might develop a line of questioning from these issues if you were the interviewer. What did Disraeli have to say on the Irish question? Are there parallels between Ireland in the 1920s and modern Bosnia? It is of course difficult to make predictions as the possibilities are numerous, but putting yourself in the interviewer's shoes is always a worthwhile exercise. It is highly likely that the PR question will be broadened into wider British constitutional issues, given the stated interest in Liberal Democrat politics. What should Britain's relation to Europe be? How should the House of Lords be reformed? How far should regional devolution go? Does this encourage nationalism? And we are neatly back to the Irish question. One advantage of having possible links between topics within your statement is that it makes it more likely

that development of the discussion will be predictable.

Read or reread Bullock's book - what would you say if you were asked what was interesting about it or what its major thrust is?

Find a couple of articles from recent copies of the Economist; read them, make notes and consider how a discussion might develop as above.

Exercise 3 - Personal details

For this exercise you should consider and then jot down the points you wish to make on your application form. Remember that you are trying to shape future interviews by offering some natural lines to the interviewer. The exercise is in two parts: the personal and the academic. For each part think about the kinds of things you need to put down to encourage desirable discussions at interview.

(a) Non-academic interests

Interest   Possible Interviewer's Questions

(b) Academic interests

Interest   Possible Interviewer's Questions

BACKGROUND TO THE INTERVIEWS

This chapter describes the role of the interview in the Oxbridge selection process and endeavours to prepare you for what to expect. Despite reassurances from totally biased and supportive parents, "Of course you will get in, darling" and encouraging teachers, "You've got as much chance as anybody else", you will probably discover that you have that familiar uncomfortable feeling in the pit of your stomach. This chapter will not necessarily cure that feeling and indeed it may in the short-term make it worse, but we hope to change the feeling of fear of the unknown to, at worst, nervous anticipation of the known. We will start by setting the context of the interviews and will then give examples of their style.

Who does the interviewing and who makes the decision?

Technical interviews are carried out by lecturers or researchers in the relevant subject who are members of the college to which you are applying. Sometimes, if insufficient numbers of these are available, someone from a different college or a different but related discipline may be used; this is rare however. Tutorial (general) interviews are usually performed by the college's admissions tutor, who has overall responsibility for running the admissions process for the college. The admissions tutor also has responsibility for making the final decision on whom to admit. They are, however, very strongly swayed by the advice of the subject experts who have interviewed you; who, after all, are the people likely to have to teach you. The admissions tutor's main role at this stage is to balance numbers between different subjects.

A report form is filled in by the interviewers; this will be used as an *aide memoire*, a means of sharing information within the college and will be sent to the Pool if necessary. Each college has its own procedure, but the report forms will all be of similar format. The interview and written work (if supplied) are separately scored on a scale of 1-10 and then an overall mark produced; however the overall mark is unlikely to be a simple average. To obtain an offer an overall mark of around 7 is required.

It should be remembered that the people who are interviewing you are likely to have little or no formal training in interviewing; they do however have many years of experience of assessing people and work in their field. The consequence of this is that they may be rather poor at some of the social skills normally associated with interviewers - establishing eye contact, being welcoming, providing feedback and giving encouragement. This is often compounded by the somewhat atypical social cross-section represented by Oxbridge lecturers. It is important to realise this and to try to avoid being fazed by the rather odd situations that you may encounter; almost all interviewers are in reality well intentioned - it just may not appear so. The appearances to the contrary are more likely caused by their inadequacy than yours; they are quite likely shy or nervous themselves (one of the authors was terrified when he interviewed for the first time).

Similarly, the rooms used for interviews are far from being designed for the purpose. They are usually the interviewers' own college rooms, the primary purpose of which will be teaching, reading, relaxing or in a few cases even living in. Thus their set-up may leave a little to be desired: chairs of odd types and placed strangely, unusual ornaments or pictures, poor lighting and so on. Again the important thing is to realise that there is no intention to make your life harder - probably it has never even occurred to the interviewers that their cosy study can become an intimidating and uncomfortable place for the candidate.

An amusing example of this type of thing is an office in one college that has only one entrance door, but, on leaving, a choice of two identical doors - one is the entrance door, the other opens into a large storage cupboard. One poor candidate, on leaving the room chose the wrong door. Unfortunately, due to nervousness and the relief of having finished the interview, rather than simply closing the door and exiting via the other one, he went right into the cupboard and closed the door behind himself before realising his mistake. This will have had absolutely no bearing on whether he was offered a place or not, but must have been an excruciating moment for the candidate.

Written work and tests

Written tests are very common in many subjects, but take a wide range of forms. Your normal A-level preparation should help you here, but we would additionally recommend looking at STEP papers for Cambridge and written tests for Oxford. Your college of first choice will give you full information of what you will be expected to do. Do not hesitate to contact them if you are unclear about any aspects. In answering these written questions, essentially the same rules apply as for technical interviews. There is perhaps rather more emphasis on factual knowledge and writing style than in the interviews. Importantly also, there is more time to think carefully and construct arguments. You are looking to produce a rather more creative answer than might be normal for schoolwork. Remember it is essential to impress rather than to avoid making mistakes. This is discussed in much more detail in following chapters. It would be worth taking any opportunities available to practise this different style of answer – perhaps your teachers can help. Very often your answers from the written tests will be picked up on and explored further in the interview. Build on your answers from the written test, but do not simply duplicate them.

You may also be asked to provide samples of your schoolwork in advance of the interviews. If possible it is worth going to special efforts to prepare one or two pieces of work of high quality and excellent presentation to fulfil this function. It is worth considering typing work if your written presentation is poor. Most colleges will inform you well in advance of what is required. Again, make a copy of what you submit and expect this work to be discussed at interview.

Getting there and deciding on what to wear

Once you have been called for interview, and virtually all applicants west of Cyprus are invited to attend for interview, your personal doubts about your suitability may well begin. Don't be put off by the formality of written communications:

Any correspondence with the college was quite sharp and abrupt. The letters were formal and gave me the impression that the whole administrative and selection process was a 'cold and callous' business. Not very confidence inspiring, I can assure you. However, the arrangements made at the college - our rooms and meals - were great. I cannot think of anything else they could have done for us.

We start by offering some straightforward 'good housekeeping' advice. What to wear is a perennial issue for interview candidates. However, the level of formality encountered is often more pronounced amongst the candidates than the interviewers:

I applied to the college because it is meant to be one of the cool, laid-back colleges (or so it said in the leaflet I was sent), but when I arrived I was shown into a really posh room with huge leather armchairs and a tray with cut-crystal glasses and pure orange, and it was full of people wearing suits and carrying briefcases. One girl had a laptop computer. I thought firstly that these were the interviewers but they were actually interviewees. They all looked really confident, except one boy who was so nervous he kept spilling orange juice on his suit.

There are two general principles we would recommend. First, it is better to look smart than shabby - no one will penalise you for making an effort, but some, probably subconsciously, will be unimpressed by excessive casualness. Second, wear something you are comfortable in - you need to make sure you give yourself the maximum chance to express your character and abilities. Many colleges will offer advice on a 'dress code'. Almost all colleges now recommend casual dress, so there is certainly no requirement to wear a jacket and tie or skirt if that makes you uncomfortable - but usually trying to look smart and competent will instil that impression in yourself and your interviewer. However, in professional subjects, Medicine and Law in particular, it is probably more important to dress in a conventionally smart manner: in some sense this is a part of the job, after all.

Another important aspect to think about as regards clothing is temperature control. Most interviews occur in December and old and poorly heated rooms abound in Oxford and Cambridge. You may also have to move between buildings during the day. Nothing is worse than shaking with cold or sweating during an interview. Having an easily removable layer is not a bad idea.

Management of your travel arrangements can be very influential. It is worth remembering that colleges will be most hospitable to students who travel some distance and will offer overnight accommodation at reasonable rates. Some colleges are particularly generous and make no charge for room or meals. There are distinct advantages in availing yourself of this offer. Apart from the obvious stress reduction of removing the worry that the 05.30 from Bristol will make the planned connection to Oxford, staying overnight will give you the opportunity to explore and get a sense of the atmosphere. This point is nicely illustrated by Tom:

> *I was pleasantly surprised to meet some fellow interviewees on the train to Cambridge. It was great to talk to people in the same boat as me. We went straight to a pub after arriving which helped us get rid of some of the loneliness. And it was a good practice for student life!*

> *I decided to walk around the town and take in the atmosphere. I thought it was important early on to decide if this was the place in which I wanted to spend three years of my life.*

The town seemed very quiet at first but there was usually a lot going on within the colleges, I was assured. I wasn't looking specifically for my college, yet I stumbled upon it before dark. Entering the college for the first time was very daunting but I was shown to my room by a very nice female student which seemed to take my mind off it! She invited me to the Student Bar to meet some of her friends and I found this extremely helpful. I would encourage anyone going for interview to talk to the students already there as well as other interviewees. I felt reassured now that I had some idea of what to expect.

This was late December. In January Tom received a conditional offer of AAB to study Law and reflected afterwards:

My first impressions were that it was a little too quiet for me, but it must be remembered that the term had ended and most students had gone home. My opinions, however, changed after I got to know some of the other interviewees. They were good fun. The people in college were extremely friendly and went out of their way to make my stay as comfortable as possible.

This offers a good example of managing the situation. Although a new and daunting experience for him, Tom made full use of both serendipitous opportunities and those offered to him by the college.

Tom's experience of a college being thoughtful and welcoming is unfortunately not always the case. Arrangements may vary; be prepared to face difficulties and discouragement such as:

> *I had been most impressed by the prospectus and looked forward to going, albeit with nervous anticipation. On arrival I found the porter arrogant and unapproachable. He spoke to me as though I was from a different civilisation. I wondered if it was me or that he was rude all the time. I located my room but found it cold and uninviting. The college was almost deserted and nobody approached me to offer words of welcome.*

We recommend arriving in Cambridge or Oxford in good time, and establishing the geography of your college and your route to and between interviews well in advance. Remember, it will be winter.

> *First tip - make good travel plans and account for weather. I ended up getting the 5.15 a.m. train from Manchester which took the best part of four hours and I had a Maths test at 10.00 a.m. I managed this OK - just. However, this, I'm afraid, is where things started really going wrong when I found that I had my first interview 30 minutes after the test finished and I had to dash around to find the room. As you can imagine I didn't do myself justice.*

You must not be late for your interview - equally

being too early can be unnerving: you may have to wait in any case as interviews often run late. Arriving ten minutes before an interview should be ample.

Make sure that your whole demeanour is business-like and sharp - any papers well filed and ordered, a familiar pen ready for action, perhaps a calculator too. All this will make little difference to the interviewers, but should give you that little edge of confidence and air of competence. It is vital to establish and maintain a positive attitude in the interview.

Interview situations

You have found the college and the interview area and are waiting to be called. What to expect? How to make an impression? It is to these questions that we now turn. There is, however, the problem of how best to offer you guidance for what will be a unique experience. To help you cope successfully with the variety of scenarios that you may have to confront, we will now provide some personal accounts, typifying the range of interview formats that might be encountered. In later chapters we will look in more detail at how to prepare for and respond to these situations.

The panel
Occasionally you may be confronted by a small panel of three or more interviewers. This situation

is most frequently encountered by medical applicants:

My first interview was in a converted loft. Sitting at a long table were three tutors. Two men and a woman, who appeared to take the lead by offering me a chair and asking if I had any problems getting here in the snow. After my polite social reply, she then asked "considering the cold conditions, how does the body maintain its temperature?". I had had to produce this answer many times before in school tests, so felt extremely relaxed as I talked about vasoconstriction, erection of body hair and shivering. This was a nice lead-in and I had no difficulty focusing on the lady who asked the question.

One of the gentlemen then showed me an electronmicrograph and asked me to describe it. At first I hadn't a clue and quickly guessed, giving some vague reason. Unfortunately, I guessed the wrong kingdom - plant instead of animal. With clues that he offered me, I then recognised the cell as a receptor-cell from the nervous system.

The other, somewhat elderly gentleman then asked me why I wanted to specialise in surgery and about advances in surgery. This was a good opportunity for me to fit in my work-experience at the local hospital. Just when I thought the interview was ending, the first gentleman showed me another electronmicrograph. This time it was a lot more difficult. I guessed again and then said I was wrong again but giving reasons for my initial guess and then for why I knew I was wrong. I never found out what it was. At one stage the lady leading the interview said my answers were of an exceptional standard but I knew that meant nothing.

The elderly gentleman then handed me a skull and pieces of another skull and asked me match the pieces. He asked to suggest why the bone was so dense around the inside of the ear, even though he knew that I hadn't studied the ear. We then talked about how sound was transmitted to the brain and about ears 'popping' in aeroplanes.

The lady thanked me and I got up to leave. I had my back to the interviewers and the door open when I heard the elderly gentleman mutter a question. I turned to face him and he asked me why Crick and Watson are important to medicine. He caught me completely by surprise but luckily I was able to put my answer together, revolving around genetically related diseases.

I went off to my next interview feeling quite happy but resolving to always be on my guard. I was delighted to get an offer of AAB five days later.

The pair

You may be confronted with a pair of interviewers. As with the panel, this situation can be unsettling if you overly concern yourself with the reactions of both interviewers. It is better to focus mainly, though not exclusively, on the interviewer who is asking the questions and not try and work out if there is some hidden psychological agenda. Similarly you should not overly concern yourself with the eminence of the interviewers. The following experience may help you to prepare for a worst case situation.

When I first arrived at the college, I, like all the other Law candidates was given a legal document. I was told to study the document carefully and that the entire first interview would be based on the document and nothing else.

I found myself apprehensive while waiting to go into the interview room, knowing that I would have to argue my patch with a world-renowned name in Law. When I entered the interview room I saw two men. One sat, if as asleep, not once looking up at me. The other sat at the opposite side of the room and seemed to be working at his desk. This one asked me to take a seat and proceeded to question me on the extract. I found it impossible to make eye contact since neither were looking at me.

One asked all the questions, the other was silent. From the start of his questioning he was intimidating. He was very patronising and dismissive of all my comments. He argued with every point I made and sometimes ridiculed them. But I stuck to my interpretation and argued with him. I did accept some of his arguments, but stuck to my point of view as much as possible and as a result the questioning became increasingly tough. This continued for about 25 minutes when he suddenly said the interview was over. The other interviewer still appeared to be asleep.

All the other candidates I spoke to found the same approach. In hindsight, I wish I had understood the document given to me more thoroughly and formulated better views and stuck to them more firmly. I felt that I let the interviewer change my mind too much. Still, I was pleased that I didn't go silent or crumble under the pressure.

The one-to-one

The most common interview situation encountered is of the single interviewer talking to a candidate. Although varying in style, the single interviewer tends to produce a more relaxed format. Most candidates prefer this model as it more closely relates to their experience of talking to one adult at a time. A fairly typical 'one-to-one' situation was faced by Anne. However, her self-conscious knowledge of body language and non-verbal communication is not something we would recommend you worry about, as it is likely to further complicate an already difficult situation.

All applicants on that day met together and received a half-hour talk from the admissions tutor about the arrangements for our interview - time and place. It was also a bit of a reassuring pep talk and not to worry too much. In between interviews we went to this room where everyone else was waiting. This was the best bit as I got to chat to all the other applicants, which was really nice. I liked them a lot but was slightly intimidated, as I was by the college, as I was pretty much convinced I wasn't good enough and wouldn't get in. All of the others seemed quite relaxed about the whole thing - they all seemed so confident and blasé about it, I thought.

The interviewers came to the room to get us and then took us to their rooms. My first interview was half an hour late. She showed me into the room and sat on a comfy chair and I sat on a matching sofa. It was very low and soft, and quite uncomfortable. I had read all this stuff about body language, about how sitting back meant you weren't interested. So I tried not to do that. I also read that crossing your arms and legs meant that you were being defensive. So I ended up feeling pretty uncomfortable and conscious of my position the whole way through the interview - as you can imagine.

The woman had a clip-board and was writing on it answers to some administrative questions she was asking me such as: "Had I considered a deferred place?" and "Was it possible at my school to do STEP papers?" She continued asking me little questions and making little notes. I felt like she wasn't so much interested in me - like she was just doing some work and I was there with her just chatting. I kind of forgot that I was being judged as I didn't get any feedback on how I was doing.

She asked me pretty much all scientific questions the whole way through: mostly biology as she was a biologist. She asked me about proteins, catalysts and chemical bonding. I did OK on the first two but I didn't know about carbon-carbon double bonds. I waffled a bit. I looked it up afterwards and found I had got it totally wrong, although I wouldn't have known from her reaction. She was always very nice and friendly and chatty but I was quite intimidated by the place and everything and I hadn't had a chance to take my coat off. With the uncomfortable sofa and now feeling very hot, it didn't make it a great experience.

Anne's second interview went well. She had learned a great deal about how to handle herself from her first experience and received an offer of AAA to study Biological Science.

There are a few points here that are worth exploring about interviews. Notice Anne's feelings of unworthiness both relative to other candidates and the college. This is extremely common; most sixth formers find it difficult to maintain their self-confidence in the face of new and intimidating surroundings. It is also almost certainly untrue; even to be at the interview you are likely to have an exceptional school record. Oxbridge gets applicants from many more able candidates than it has places available; if you are offered a place, you will very likely cope well with your chosen course and benefit from the experience. When feeling small, try to bear these points in mind and, like Anne, concentrate on the job in hand rather than worrying about whether you are good enough - it is after all the interviewers' job to decide that.

Anne's interview was almost entirely technical. This is very common and even when there is a more general interview or significant numbers of questions on your personal interests, the point of overriding importance will be your performance on the technical material.

Finally notice that Anne got some things wrong in her interview (the carbon-carbon double bonds) and yet got an offer. Again this is normal. It is fairly rare for candidates to go through all their interviews making no errors or showing no misconceptions; you are after all being pushed to the limits of your knowledge and ability by experts in the field. What will get you in is not consistent lack of errors, but showing an ability to think clearly and logically and having a quick, flexible and imaginative mind. This need only happen for part of an interview to be sufficient to impress.

Exercise 4 - Interview technique

As you can see from the above introductory examples, it is difficult to prepare for the Oxbridge interview. Indeed it can be a mistake to be overly conscious of how you appear. It is better to be yourself and to think about the questions rather than wonder if your body posture is correct. Nevertheless, are there any personal lessons that you can learn from the above illustrations? We suggest that you take some time at this point to make notes which might help in your preparations for when you 'receive the call'.

THE PERSONAL INTERVIEW

The personal interview is the classic of Oxbridge mythology, in which the young physics candidate's future hangs in the balance as he struggles to define the third person of the Trinity or offer some new insight into the fall of the British Empire, preferably in Latin. Times have changed, and the modern personal interview will be down to earth (and in English!). Indeed, not all colleges will engage in a separate personal interview, and in any case it will primarily be the technical discussions that count. However, the personal interview may be influential in distinguishing candidates where marginal differences must be finely sifted. Where there is a personal interview, the interviewer will try to assess such attributes as motivation, interest in the subject and possible contributions to college life. Insights will also be gained into a candidate's background and school. These may assist when trying to assess potential, rather than achievements alone.

The experience of the personal interview recounted below is fairly typical:

My first interview was general and conducted by the admissions tutor. He asked me a general question about my journey to Cambridge and then asked me why I had applied to this particular college. I was also asked questions about the Single European

Currency, global warming and questions about information contained in my UCAS form and personal application form. Generally, I felt as though he was trying to find out if I had opinions of my own and was reasonably well informed on current affairs.

This rather gentle chat lasted for half an hour. Usually personal interviews take place prior to technical interviews and it is a useful way for candidates to become acquainted with the interview situation. It is also possible for the personal interview to be replaced by a questionnaire administered by the college, prior to the interviews. Treat this seriously:

On the morning of the interview there was a briefing session for interviewees of all subjects. We were told where to wait and what time our interview was. We were also handed forms to fill out. Firstly, our own details and education then on our families; our siblings' education and ages and our parents' education and occupations - also if any of our families are graduates. The second part asked why we wanted to go to university, why we chose this particular college, and would we be willing to take an offer of deferred entry. After this briefing we went to the waiting room. My interview was two hours later.

Where a personal interview is held, you should be on your guard, as the subject matter may rapidly become technical:

I was informed that this would be a general interview, but I encountered very few general questions. I was forced to give very brief answers to questions such as: Why Engineering? Why Oxford? Why this college? The majority of the interview was spent discussing the mathematical properties of circles.

Such instances are not uncommon and find their echo in the frequent appearance of "general" questions as a prelude to many technical interviews. It is also worth remembering that what passes for small talk among Mathematics dons is very likely to be the mathematical properties of circles. On a more serious note, as a considerable portion of your time at university will be spent immersed in your chosen subject and in the company of fellow students, a genuine interest in discussing your subject outside of the required syllabus is essential. This makes it seem entirely natural in an Oxbridge context for technical material to creep into any general discussion.

The following sequence of questions encountered by a candidate for architecture is a typical example of combining the personal with the technical.

Why did you choose this college in particular?
What do you think of the college so far?
What clubs and societies would you join here?
Why do you want to be an architect?
How are your A-level subjects related to one another?

What type of books do you like to read?
What was the last book you read? (I answered
'Swan Song' - a book about nuclear disaster).
If there were a nuclear war, would you attempt
to reconstruct the style of buildings that had
been destroyed or try a new style?
How is the hierarchy in your school related to
that of the government?
What was involved in your work experience?
How is dancing related to architecture?
What sort of buildings are there in your home
town?
Have you any favourites?

Some of these questions such as those dealing with choice of college and subject are predictable. Others spring up in the course of the conversation, which is frequently guided by the interviewer onto the candidate's subject area. Usually, the questioning will be confined to your choice of college, choice of subject and personal interests. School experiences, future career and current affairs are also common topics of conversation.

Why this college?

Assuming you have not applied by Open Application, there must be some reasons why you have chosen your college. Most interviewers like to feel their university, and their college in particular, has a unique character and something special to offer. Many put a lot of effort into their college life. In answering this question you should not mention tactical considerations, such as numbers or perceived quality of applicants. However, if a part of the reason is that your school does not have experience with STEP papers and the college has expressed a willingness to allow for this, then by all means mention it as part of your reason. You would also be advised not to include caveats about your choice that may offend the interviewer ("I suppose it is a bit run down and old fashioned but..."). It is unlikely that you will really know what it is like to be at a particular college until you study there, but providing evidence that you have carefully considered the question, such as mentioning sources of information you have read or open days attended is recommended. The notes you will have made in the chapter on 'Choosing your College' will be most helpful in preparing you to answer this question.

Why study this subject?

Questions as to why candidates wish to study their chosen subjects are ubiquitous. The interviewer will be trying to assess whether the candidates have a genuine interest and enthusiasm for their subject, and have thought carefully about what it entails. Once at university, the student will have to work independently and be self-motivated. Follow-up questions are also very likely to include why a related subject was not chosen. For example, why choose Classics rather than Archaeology or why Engineering rather than Physics? The interviewer may also ask if you have considered deferring, or whether a similar course at another university would be better suited to your interests. In instances where there is choice of options or modules, the candidate is often asked which of these they plan to study. Of course, most candidates will not have a clear idea of their intentions in detail and, in any case, will not be held to any decisions they make. However it is important to show that you have thought about the degree structure on offer, and preferably have looked closely at the content of the course to make sure it interests you and that your expectations of it are realistic.

A related question is what the candidate intends to do after graduating - some indication of this may already have been made on the application form, and this is the chance to demonstrate that you have thought further about possible careers than the fifteen words written. For many subjects studied it is acceptable and normal to have no fixed views on this, and a flat "no" will do no harm. In professionally oriented subjects, such as Medicine or Law, it is important to have a realistic knowledge of how the professions operate and where you see your career developing within them.

Candidates are also frequently asked why they enjoy studying their subjects at school, if they have favourite areas and how they organise their work. It is common to be asked to comment on past performance at exams and explain any imperfections. There is an element of chance in all exams, and there may be genuine mitigating circumstances that you can point out. It is important to remain positive, and it comes across better to take responsibility for yourself and show that you have learned from the results, rather than to blame others or circumstances beyond your control. Similarly, display confidence, if necessary erring on the side of optimism, when asked what grades you expect to get in your future exams. British candidates might need to practise this overt optimism in front of a mirror!

Personal interests and current affairs

The interviewer is likely to ask questions on any interests or experience mentioned in the application form. This is an opportunity to show you have a life outside your subject and could make a contribution to the college environment. It is important not to contradict anything you have written. The days when sporting prowess alone could guarantee entrance have passed, but high achievements in any activity, sporting or otherwise, will impress. Instances where the candidate and interviewer share a common interest are a good opportunity to build a rapport. Candidates may find that this is the first time in their lives that they have had to talk about themselves in this personal way; avoid reticence. A mock interview provides an opportunity to hear oneself and may make this dialogue much easier to maintain, even if the topics discussed prove to be very different. Questions on topical events and current affairs are also popular. Be clear that what is being looked for is not whether you have the 'right' opinions, but whether you have opinions at all and can articulate them. Do not be afraid to be controversial, but be prepared to back up what you say with rational arguments.

Other issues

The law with respect to most job interviews requires that the questions asked to each candidate should not be different solely because of the interviewee's gender or race. Expect no such niceties at Oxbridge. While in an ideal world we might expect the interviewer to be blind to race or gender, in practice a girl applying for medicine might be asked how she expects to succeed in such a male-dominated profession. A student from Northern Ireland will almost inevitably be asked their opinions on the political situation there. The best advice is to use these as opportunities for stimulating discussion that may genuinely interest the interviewer and help you stand out from the crowd. If you feel genuinely offended by something the interviewer asks then by all means muster the confidence to point out and explain why you feel the interviewer is being unfair - most academics like to argue and be challenged. However be careful not to come across as overly sensitive or self-righteous. Maintaining, or at least feigning, a sense of humour is advised.

Closing the interview

At the conclusion of most interviews, the candidates are invited to ask questions of their own. This is an occasion of considerable and quite unnecessary discomfort for many candidates:

> *She then invited me to ask her some questions. I asked her a question on the college's facilities which she answered, and then asked if I had any other questions. This surprised me and I panicked, before managing to quickly think of another question. After answering this question she again asked me if I had any other questions, and I managed to ask her about something she had said in her second answer. When she finished answering this she again asked me if I had another question to which I replied I hadn't, and left. My advice to future applicants would be to prepare more than one question.*

Better advice still is not to persevere with questions that you don't really want answered. It is likely to come across as artificial, and an admissions tutor concluding the sixth interview of the day can become weary where proceedings are protracted unnecessarily. Do not ask a question which is readily answered by the college or subject prospectus - you have read them, haven't you? Personal questions of the interviewer ("So do you like it here?") should also be avoided unless you have struck up a surprisingly rapid rapport.

However this part of the interview is a good opportunity to discuss issues where the information is not available elsewhere or which require clarification, and to bring up genuine concerns you may have. Most candidates do feel obliged to have at least one question available, and on the whole we advise you to have something prepared in the eventuality that you feel under pressure to ask a question. The intricacies of the Oxbridge system leave room to seek interpretation on a range of issues such as subject choices, transfers, facilities and so forth.

Exercise 5 - Topics for discussion

(a) You should have already constructed some notes for answers to the standard questions concerning your choice of college. Now take time to make notes on why you wish to study your chosen subject and what aspects of the course appeal to you.

(b) How do you see yourself in five years' time?

(c) It is quite likely that you will be engaged in conversation about topical issues, especially those which relate to your subject area. Close to your interview, we suggest you make headings below of topical issues which may be discussed during your interview at Oxbridge.

(d) Make notes here of what questions, if any, you wish to ask at the end of your interview.

THE TECHNICAL INTERVIEW

The so-called 'technical interview' is the most important aspect of the selection process. Although other aspects have a part to play in determining who is selected and contribute to the overall picture, the technical interview provides colleges with their primary decision-making information. The criteria employed to assist interviewers in this process will be interpreted differently from subject to subject but nevertheless possess some general qualities. The technical interview will be designed to examine your ability to think on your feet and your aptitude to tackle new problems. The interviewers will attempt to understand the quality of your thought processes by seeing if you can reason carefully and logically and employ critical and analytical skills. They will also look for creativity, flair and a display of intellectual curiosity. Through your answers they will additionally hope to assess if you have a genuine interest in your chosen subject, are self-motivated and have a determination to excel in your field.

Assessment criteria

We have identified three criteria generally used by interviewers in their assessments. We will now do our best to introduce these criteria and, through some specific examples, show you how these are applied by the college interviewers in their selection processes.

Understanding and knowing your school work

Understanding and knowledge of your school work are necessary but insufficient requirement for a successful interview. It will be assumed that you have a good grasp of GCSE and A level subject matter. The primary purpose of the technical interview is not to test this knowledge, although it may well provide the starting point for the discussions. It will be recognised that you may have only completed half of your A-level programme of studies. It is essential in this early part of the technical interview that you do not undermine your candidature by making errors or displaying unforgivable gaps in your knowledge. Trivial slips due to nervousness would be understood and should not be a cause for worry. If you spot these, simply correct them as soon as possible. You may well find the interviewer correcting them for you. You should see your subject knowledge as a basic tool with which you will begin to forge your answers to new and more interesting questions. For example, you will need to 'know' basic calculus to carry out analysis of physical problems and mistakes in your basic knowledge could well be damning to your chances. Similarly, familiarity with set texts in English or periods in History would be assumed.

It will also be assumed that you understand and, crucially, are able to explain the underlying principles of your subjects, and this is very likely to form the start of further analysis.

Interest in your subject beyond the syllabus and its application in wider contexts

It is important to demonstrate a broader interest in your school subject topics than that explored within the narrow confines of the syllabus and examination requirements. In cases where the subject you have applied to read is not represented by your A-level studies, such as Philosophy, Law, Medicine and Architecture, it is of even greater importance that you are able to demonstrate an awareness of ideas beyond school subject interests. Such interests may be manifested by your ability to discuss your readings from journals and relevant general literature in the field or in your ability to apply the concepts and knowledge learnt at school to the analysis of everyday situations. For example, is it possible to find some parallels between German unification in the late nineteenth century and modern European integration, or use your physics to decide whether melting ice caps will affect the sea level?

Your thought processes

How do you think? Understanding and evaluating your intellectual equipment is the most important stage in the assessment of your abilities and potentials. In a sense, all that has taken place up until this point is a preparation for exploring your fundamental intellectual qualities. Oxbridge interviewers will explore the extent to which you can think originally about unfamiliar problems and ideas. This will involve you attempting to develop logically an abstract concept or argument in unfamiliar territory. The nature of the concept or argument will vary considerably from subject to subject but there remains this common theme running through all Oxbridge interviews. Essentially what the interviewers are trying to do is bring out and lay bare your thought processes. This can be a traumatic experience. However, to try and avoid this situation by defensive and non-committal responses will usually bring about your failure. Indeed, you must look on this experience positively by recognising that your increasing discomfort is often an indicator of the interviewer's increasing interest in you as a serious candidate.

Perceptions

How we see the world does not necessarily correspond to how others may view it. In the interview situation this is heightened by the clear distinction of two parties with differing objectives. One is interested in showing themselves in the best possible light. The other is primarily interested in gaining a tolerably full understanding of the other's qualities. We find frequently that even very good candidates become insecure and, at times, even despondent during the interview when things are seemingly going very badly. That the interviewer has consciously constructed the circumstance of the insecurity is usually not fully appreciated by the candidate. The purpose of this section is to help you understand these circumstances and point the way towards recovery and a positive outlook.

The most frequent feeling is that correct answers are ignored and confusion is driven home.

Certainly a good answer is often moved on from quickly (but not ignored) whilst it is very common to repeatedly help candidates through problems they are confused by - this often provides useful insight into thought processes. This may produce an impression of vindictiveness, but results simply from the need to use a short period of time efficiently. Similarly there seems little point in spending a lot of time trying to impress the candidate or inform them about Oxbridge, if you are going to reject most anyway and only half an hour is available for assessment. The admissions process absorbs a significant amount of busy people's time and there is a strong incentive to minimise this.

Feelings of disorientation and intellectual inadequacy should be viewed positively as a demonstration of the interviewer's belief in your potential. Interviewers are not engaged in a desire to humiliate and disconcert. They have a short period of time in which to gain insight into your intellectual capabilities and will press you hard if they are seriously interested. This will make it difficult for you to accurately assess how things are going. Unless you are a potential Nobel Prize winner you should only worry if you haven't been stretched to a feeling of incapacity to think clearly.

Another point is that to succeed in impressing the interviewer it is not enough to avoid making errors. You will need to produce some golden nuggets of excellence. The 'conservative' approach is unlikely to impress, unlike in an A-level examination where avoiding mistakes and answering all the questions guarantees success. You need to be prepared to 'stick your neck out' and take a risk when displaying your thought processes. Beware, however, not to lose sight of utilising your basic knowledge. In this context, taking a risk does not mean guessing: that is usually disastrous. It means having the courage to express your own ideas and getting stuck in to areas where you are unsure of the answer. Remember you need to convince the interviewer that you would be an exciting and interesting person to teach. This is an interactive process. It is important that you take an active rather than passive role. Nobody wants to teach an undergraduate afraid to contribute his or her ideas in a tutorial situation.

In summary, we suggest that you always try to be positive throughout your interview. Do not become overly concerned when you find yourself struggling to answer progressively more probing technical questions. Be outgoing, take an active part in the discussion and contribute your own ideas.

Preparation

There is a profound sense in which one cannot be fully prepared for an interview. The content is fundamentally unpredictable and success depends primarily upon responding well to the situation at the time. Also, and perhaps particularly in applying to Oxbridge, you may end up across the table from an eccentric. One candidate for Oriental Studies for example was asked what she thought of a pile of pebbles for a garden, the interviewer declaring he was opposed in principle to gardens; another in English arrived to find his two interviewers busily engaged on their washing up. No amount of preparation is going to assist you in this type of situation - perhaps that was the aim, but then again perhaps the rarefied Oxbridge air had altered perceptions of reality. That said, most interviews are not like this; there is at least some element of predictability and careful preparation can make a big difference.

We divide preparation into two categories: the superficial and the substantial. The superficial generally concerns organisational and presentational issues: these are important, chiefly in terms of making you feel relaxed and giving you the best platform from which to express yourself - they will not on the whole make a tangible difference to the content or progress of the interview itself. The substantial issues are your opportunity to predict and affect the progress of the interview.

Superficial
These concern such issues as dress and organisation, and have been covered previously. One anecdote should serve to emphasise that these matters are important to get right from the point of view of your own comfort and confidence. A young lecturer in Social Psychology was interviewing for the first time a few years ago. Being keen to make his candidates feel as comfortable as possible, he gave them a choice of four chairs; a low comfortable

armchair, a high-backed chair, a wicker chair and a sofa. Unfortunately, the candidates were aware of issues in psychology and sociology and also knew that the fraction of successful candidates in the subject was about one in four; many leapt to the conclusion that choosing the correct chair was an important test when they entered the room! This hardly served to put them at their ease as had been intended. The moral of this story should be that it is worth doing all you can in your preparations to ensure that you feel comfortable and are not ambushed by the unexpected. However, inevitably the unexpected does happen - on the whole this sort of superficial issue is only important in so far as it worries you; if you can avoid being fazed, no substantive consequences will result.

Substantial
We have already discussed how you can use the information requested on the application form to manipulate the course of the interview. It really is very likely that you will be asked questions relating to what you wrote on the form and it is therefore essential that you are ready for this. Read your photocopy of the form before the interview and make sure you are prepared. Read the books you claim to have read and prepare a little to say on topics you have declared interest in. It also will do no harm to consider how a line of questioning might develop from these topics - you never know, you might strike lucky!

There is considerably more preparation needed beyond revising your application form. Often samples of your schoolwork are requested, such as practical write-ups in Science, essays in History or English. This is partly to assess the quality of your written work (and your school), but also to provide lead-ins for further questioning. You must ensure that you are fully on top of the written work you have provided and are able to discuss it both in a broader context and from different perspectives. If you have done a practical on swinging pendulums, be ready to derive the equation of simple harmonic motion; if you have written an essay on monetary policy under Thatcher, be prepared to contrast it to a Keynesian model of reflation. Choose the pieces of work you submit on this basis and try to keep the scope available to the interviewers to a minimum, within the confines of providing what is requested.

There are some very common questions that it would be foolish not to have an answer ready for:

Choose a topic from your course-work that is of particular interest to you. Choose something you have done recently, feel thoroughly confident of and preferably have a real interest in - context beyond the course would be very desirable too.

Is there a discovery/piece of literature/historical event you are particularly excited by? Choose something of genuine interest/significance but of sufficiently limited scope and simple theory that you have a good chance of discussing it coherently. Mendel's peas or the withdrawal from the Gold Standard might be good examples.

Do you read regularly literature of relevance to your subject? You must answer yes! But it needn't be the Hungarian Journal of Post-modern Iconography: the Economist, New Scientist, London Review of Books or even relevant newspaper articles are fine. Make sure you can explain one or two recent articles in reasonable depth.

We have given some specific advice, but there is no substitute for thinking for yourself. Put yourself in the interviewers' shoes - imagine you wanted to test your imagination, ability to think beyond your school work and enthusiasm for your subject: what would you ask? For every item you are required to supply (schoolwork, personal statement, application forms, etc.) think what supplementary questions could be asked and try to manipulate the information available to optimal effect.

Most interviewers are aiming to give you the chance to express yourself at your best in areas of interest to you. They are likely to give you quite a lot of opportunities to achieve this - make sure you use those opportunities to the full: interviewers will happily set the agenda if you fail to and that is likely to make life harder for you.

General advice

Here we give some tips on things that are difficult to do in interviews because they appear awkward or unnatural, but which are generally useful or appear impressive to the interviewer. Before jumping into answering questions, try to think about one or two of these points.

Do be prepared to stop and think - silences appear awkward but are OK. Nothing is more impressive than a candidate pausing to consider and then producing an intelligent remark. Don't feel obliged to always jump straight in - if necessary say you would just like to think about that point for a few seconds.

Be prepared to interrupt the interviewers. Often they will start trying to give you some hint or assistance if they feel you are on the wrong track. If at any point you suddenly realise what on earth they are on about, feel free to get in as soon as possible. Similarly if you disagree with something they are talking about, say so: but don't be overly dogmatic about it.

Use a pen or pencil to start to develop your ideas. This is particularly important in more mathematical disciplines: often you can start to develop a solution on paper even if you are unclear where the final solution is heading. If you start to write something down or draw a picture of the problem, it gives you time to think

Be prepared to say you don't understand something: it is disastrous to start guessing. No one expects you to know everything and anyway the question may be clearer if rephrased. Often expressing ignorance will lead you straight onto a different topic rather than wallowing for ages in something you know nothing about. Of course you can't say you don't understand everything!

Make sure you answer questions accurately and concisely - don't waffle and flounder. Expanding into other interesting areas is fine, but only after you have shown a good command of the initial question. Avoid being vague or making generalisations you cannot substantiate. Use examples in your answers.

Make connections to other subjects you know about and to other topics covered in the interview. Often interviewers will ask successive questions on seemingly unrelated but actually linked topics to try to test just this skill. It is important to be able to grasp the connections between different areas of a subject.

In Humanities, courage in expressing, and modifying, a view on your own initiative will be seen as a valuable quality.

Case studies

We will now present you with four detailed case studies, the first a complete example and the next three forming exercises. These studies should illustrate many of the points made above and also in previous chapters. Make sure you read them critically, bearing in mind all that you have already learned.

Case Study 1 - English Literature

I had two interviews and a written test given the evening before.

There was a waiting room with coffee and lots of students to answer any questions about Cambridge, the college and the English course. Everyone was very friendly and welcoming - I encountered no snobbery.

The written test was actually a blessing in disguise as it gave eight or nine English applicants a chance to bond. I felt immediately at home with most of them.

Each interview was held in the room of the respective interviewer and I had the use of a map to find them. It was very, very scary sitting outside the interview rooms. However, inside the atmosphere was as relaxed as it could be - I had somehow envisaged a grey room with a metal table and a bare bulb. But the set up was comfortable and not in the least intimidating.[1]

The first interview revolved almost entirely around a poem I was given to read. It was much more subject - based than I had expected.[2]

The poem was a sonnet about hunting and I remember that he initially asked me my opinion about the fox hunting debate in parliament. I immediately started waffling on about how I thought it was merely a case of Labour trying to seem different to their predecessors. He agreed but then accused me of not actually answering the question.[3] Ouch! The rest of the interview was a step-by-step guided analysis of the poem. I couldn't remember what 'hind' meant. It must have been nerves, and made me feel very stupid. [4]

There was no feedback that I can remember. I felt the interviewer to be rather cold.

My second interview had a much more positive feel to it. The interviewer asked me one or two questions about some essays I had had to send in advance.[5]

Next I had to read an extract aloud. It had been written by a child (although I wasn't told until afterwards) and had little punctuation or grammar. We talked about whether or not the gender of a writer is important. I felt as if I had scored points here because I was able to mention a book ("Grace Notes" by Bernard MacLaverty) which the interviewer hadn't yet read, in which the male author writes from a frighteningly convincing female perspective.[6] That gave me a real confidence boost because I recommended it to her. On the whole I felt much better about this interview than the first. She asked me what I thought I would get in my A-Levels, and if there was anything I wished I had said in my first interview. I mentioned the 'hind' fiasco.[7]

After the second interview I was on a high (partly because the whole thing was over!). I had no idea how I had done, but I felt that no matter what happened, I had had an enriching experience. I was keener than ever to go to the college.

Between interviews I was just nervous. I felt that I could have had more preparation, but also that you can never really prepare for something like this. It's best not to expect anything. The normality of Cambridge should be stressed. I arrived expecting to be surrounded by eggheads and people with titles. It amazed me that everyone I met was so down to earth.

Comments on Case Study 1

1. Interviewers usually attempt to make the surroundings relaxing. However, most people find the experience of waiting outside the interview room a nerve-racking one, and you should therefore avoid arriving excessively early.

2. It is not unusual for all interviews to be subject-based, and for a supposedly general interview to quickly become technical.

3. The candidate has been asked an unexpected

and difficult question, which forces her to express opinions of her own and is hard to answer without the possibility of causing offence to someone. However, it is much better to be controversial than to be vague. Not answering a question, or answering a different question is also a serious error - in this case the candidate realises this and does not make the same mistake again.

4. In the circumstances, the best advice is to admit that you can't remember the meaning of the word, confidently ask to be reminded, and proceed without worrying. While damaging to your confidence this is quite a common circumstance and should not be nearly as damning as the candidate imagines. The important thing is to be able to complete the analysis of the poem: guessing and attempting to bluff would be far more dangerous.

5. Questions on any written work provided by the candidate are to be expected, and present a good opportunity for the well-prepared candidate to shine.

6. This is a very important moment in the interview. The candidate has demonstrated her interest in literature outside of the school syllabus, has thought about it independently and is able to discuss it analytically, intelligently and in depth. Occasions where the interviewer learns something of interest represent a strong plus which will help you stand out from the crowd.

7. The candidate takes the opportunity to correct a previous mistake. This is a good decision, as the different interviewers will meet to discuss the case afterwards. In addition the candidate has the satisfaction of having done her best.

Case Study 2 - Natural Sciences

My technical interview was conducted by a physicist and a chemist. I was only expecting one interviewer and found this duet more unnerving. They began by asking me about the subjects I was thinking of taking in the first year on the Natural Sciences Tripos and did I read any journal like the New Scientist to which I replied "sometimes!". They then asked me to tell them about some important recent breakthrough in physics.

I hadn't prepared for this question and I chose to discuss nuclear fusion for the simple reason that I didn't know about anything else. I explained that we had not yet covered the nuclear physics section of the course so I knew about it in general terms. I failed to answer a series of questions about the workings of a nuclear reactor and the principles of nuclear fusion. I found his persistence in this area very difficult to handle as I told him that I knew little about it and eventually the subject was changed. By this time I was feeling uncomfortable and couldn't wait until it was over.

At this point the interviewer looked through my laboratory book which I had been asked to bring to the interview. He asked me to talk about the graph on the breaking point of steel illustrating Hooke's Law, which he had found in the book. He asked me more in-depth questions on the behaviour of the actual atoms in the steel wire than I had previously considered.

We then 'discussed' the production of notes on strings and the factors which affect this. I then had to do a problem on dimensions on paper which they watched. I actually felt much more confident about working things out on paper and I made sure that I explained everything out loud as I went along so that they could see my 'logical' train of thought. Although I was on quite firm ground, my feeling was that throughout this discussion they had had to drag things out of me.

They asked me what area of Physics I was interested in and when I said mechanics they gave me a problem with a table tennis ball and a small rubber ball being bounced on a table at the same time. I had to explain what was happening and why. The physics tutor said that I had got it basically correct but by that point I was sure that I had blown it and it did not seem to matter.

I also professed an interest in 'Light' and was handed a lump of crystal and asked about how waves could be used with this. He was obviously referring to X-ray diffraction. While not on the syllabus I said I knew of its uses and that it had been employed in trying to determine the structure of DNA. Of course they then asked about the structure of DNA and what was special about it.

Throughout the interview I got the impression that the two interviewers were trying hard not to laugh at me. I felt that they would glance at each other when I said something and would look disbelieving when I made a mistake.

The whole way through the interview I just wanted to get out and I felt tongue-tied and basically rather thick. When I left the interview all I wanted to do was to leave the college and never go back. It was with great surprise therefore that I received an offer. The school got some feedback which stated that I reasoned well and shown clarity of thought and 'eloquence'! It still sounds like a different interview to me. On reflection I now realise that they had been trying to see how I reacted under pressure.

Exercise 6

Make your own critical comments on this interview. We suggest you use the same style as in Case Study 1. Compare with our comments that follow.

Comments on Exercise 6

1. The candidate mentions he reads New Scientist sometimes - he should be prepared to discuss an article he has read recently.

2. The discussion of nuclear fusion is a disaster. While the candidate did show some awareness of work in the subject outside the syllabus, he made the cardinal error of suggesting a topic on which he was ill prepared. It is very hard to have a sensible discussion on nuclear fusion without knowledge of the basic principles. The candidate should have anticipated this question, whereupon he could have directed the discussion onto an area where he could do himself justice, and have some foundation to build on when he was inevitably drawn into deeper waters.

3. The switch to more familiar ground on an experiment covered in school provides an opportunity to recover. However, the interview moves quickly into areas beyond the syllabus.

4. The candidate, while downhearted, begins a revival by demonstrating his competence at maths. Writing gives time to think and restores an air of confidence - sensibly he remembers to discuss his reasoning.

5. The candidate feels the interviewers must 'drag things out' - be more active in the discussion to avoid this. Try and fill the gaps.

6. The question on explaining properties of bouncing balls is a classic interview question. An answer should involve applying concepts of conservation of energy and momentum to explain the motion seen. Further discussion could include the molecular properties of the materials that allow them to bounce.

6. In the case of the crystal, the interviewers were probably expecting him to talk about refraction of light, a standard school physics topic. The candidate has showed some creativity in choosing to talk about X-ray diffraction and doing so competently. Bringing in knowledge of its application to the discovery of DNA structure was also a plus.

7. Typically the candidate feels he has 'blown it' at an early stage - remember this is not a driving test.

He also feels he is being 'laughed at'. Importantly, however, this does not stop him trying his best during his interview.

Case Study 3 - Law

I applied to study Law. My first interview was with Mr A. I was surprised at how relaxed I felt just before the interview. The interview began well. Mr A. seemed to be genuinely interested in my interests and future plans. His attitude, however, changed once he began to talk about matters concerning the Law. At times he appeared uninterested in my responses and got quite aggressive when he did not agree with what I was saying. He asked me about the Lord Chancellor and I talked about this in depth, highlighting a possible conflict of interest with his position on the Cabinet. He then asked me to define privacy. I tried to answer the question but he continued to interrupt me arguing that I was avoiding the question and that if I did not know the answer, just admit it. At this point I was angry and frustrated but managed to control myself and explain that if he had let me finish I would have answered the question. I then went on to define privacy correctly and he seemed impressed. He also asked me a lot of shorter questions on things like Law of Tort and Constitutional Law etc. I found this interview quite intense and felt under a great deal of pressure to give answers quickly. I later found that many of the other interviewees thought that Mr A. was demanding. The interview passed very quickly and then it was time to take the written test.

I found the written test fairly straightforward. We were told to be as analytical as possible. Here is an example of the type of questions set - it may be of some use to you. No previous legal knowledge is required.

"Murder is when someone, with the intention of causing death or serious bodily harm, does an act which causes the death of another person."

In each case decide whether X is guilty of murder or not. Give reasons for your answer.

X holds a grudge against Y. He sets fire to the house of Y knowing that he is at home. Y tries to escape the flames by jumping out the bedroom window but is killed by the fall. Is X guilty of murder?

X and Z have a huge argument. Filled with anger, X grabs Z by the throat and strangles her. He is full of remorse when he sees the unconscious body of Z. Believing her to be dead already, he attempts to get rid of the body by throwing it in the river. Z, however, had only been unconscious and dies through drowning. Is X guilty of murder?

X poisons some chocolates and gives then to Y, intending to poison him. Y, however, unknowingly gives the chocolates to Z. Z eats the chocolates and dies from poisoning. Is X guilty of murder?

I don't think they were looking for correct answers but the ability to analyse and interpret the Law, and to argue your case logically.

On the same day myself and three other Law candidates were called for a second interview quite late in the evening. It was with a law tutor from another college. On coming to the college we were given the case study of a young man who ended up in a vegetative state after the Hillsborough Stadium tragedy.

After being given insufficient time to read the document I was called for the interview with Mr B. He then asked me to lecture him on the case study which I had just read. I found this difficult to begin with since I did not know where to start. This lasted for 10 minutes. He then did a tutorial with me on the subject of lies and white lies which lasted about 5 minutes. He said he was doing this to find out what I would be like in a student-tutor relationship.

The third interview, with Mrs C., was much more relaxed. She was extremely friendly and very easy to talk to. She asked a few of the questions for which I was prepared, e.g. Why did I choose to apply here and to study Law? She then went on to talk about very general topics which had been in the news recently. She asked what I knew about the recent Climate Summit and I was luckily well informed on this topic. It proves that it is invaluable to keep up with current affairs and formulate your own ideas on each issue. We both came to the conclusion that the developed world should first try and raise the standard of living in developing countries before imposing environmental restrictions upon them. Mrs C. wondered what I intended to do after receiving a Law degree. I said that I was keeping my options open but that I had seriously considered becoming a solicitor rather than a barrister because I would enjoy dealing with clients on a more personal basis. She then quizzed me on whether I thought there was a need for the two separate professions. I suggested the introduction of some type of advocate who would oversee the case from the very start as well as appearing in court. She seemed to be in full agreement with this idea. The interview concluded with a chat about my interests with particular reference to my interest in choral and instrumental music. The only questions I asked at the end of the interview were with regard to the different sports and, more importantly, "night-time" activities available at the college.

When my interviews were over I did not think that I had done myself justice, particularly in the interview with Mr A. I thought that I got a little too flustered and annoyed at his interviewing style. However, after speaking to the other interviewees it was obvious that it had been the same for everyone. In fact after hearing how some of them did I began to feel a little more confident about how I performed.

I received a conditional offer to study Law.

Exercise 7

Make your own critical comments on this interview. We suggest you use the same style as in Case Study 1. Compare with our comments that follow.

Comments on Exercise 7

1. Discussion of the role of the Lord Chancellor showed knowledge of law outside the school syllabus and that the candidate had opinions of his own. In vocational subjects such as Law and Engineering, knowledge of professional aspects is important.

2. The candidate did well on the incident surrounding the definition of privacy by standing up to the aggressive interviewer. Crucially, the candidate kept a clear head and came up with a good answer to the question.

3. In this interview speed of thought and ability to argue was also being tested. It is important to keep thinking about answers when under pressure, and avoid being pushed (or bullied) into a rash response. This is particularly true of Law where quick thinking under aggressive questioning is a part of the job.

4. In the written tests, as the candidate points out, a simple 'yes' or 'no' answer to each question will not impress. Answering requires careful thought, discussion of the issues and articulation of the arguments backing up your conclusions. Remember however that it is always helpful, if not vital, to give correct or convincing answers.

5. In discussing the answers there is a particular emphasis on verbal articulation of ideas. This is a skill that can be greatly improved by practising, but

is not often developed at school where the emphasis is on written answers.

6. The 'tutorial' session is an explicit example of what most interviewers will want to know - how you will fare in the particular circumstances of the Oxbridge tutorial system. This also gives the interviewer an indication of the student's ability to assimilate new ideas rapidly.

Case Study 4 - Chemical Engineering

I had two interviews, first a general one and then a longer subject one.

Interview 1
My first interview was at 4.45 with the admissions tutor, Dr D. The interview was held in her flat in the college. I sat down on a couch while she sat opposite in an armchair. She asked me a lot of questions on the subjects that I was studying for A-Level including:

- something I found interesting in each of my subjects;
- how strong I was in each of the subjects;
- how well equipped each science department in my school was;
- how would I persuade a younger pupil of my school to study Chemistry (which I had already mentioned was my best subject).

I was asked why I had picked Chemical Engineering. I replied that I wished to keep studying Chemistry in some form and I also wished to be an engineer so it seemed logical to pick Chemical Engineering. She then asked me if I read any scientific magazines. I replied that I sometimes read the New Scientist. I was then asked to tell her about an interesting article that I had read, so I told her about the invention of a special type of biological 'bullet' which could be used to cure cancer, and mentioned that Chemical Engineers were actually involved in developing the material which was going to be used in the bullet.

I felt that the interview went well as I had been able to answer all her questions without too much trouble. It was really just an informal chat with nothing too demanding being asked.

Interview 2
This was at 5.30 and was again held in the interviewer's flat. The interviewer was Dr E. who informed me that he was particularly interested in me because I had applied to do Chemical Engineering and he was a Chemical Engineering tutor.

He first of all asked me about an Engineering project that I had done involving the manufacture of Viscose. I had prepared for questions on this by bringing a sample of Viscose to Cambridge and by learning how Viscose is manufactured from the manufacturer's information booklet. He said he wasn't familiar with Viscose, so I attempted to show him the sample I had brought but to my horror I discovered that I had left it in my room, so I had to describe the process which contained some terms that I only half understood such as monofilament and spinning cells. I was relieved when I managed to bluff my way through. He then asked me a bit about my work experience, especially about P & I diagrams (which I had mentioned on my form).

He then asked me to tell him about some areas in which Chemical Engineers work. I mentioned that they were trying to find ways of reducing pollution. He then asked me how sulphur dioxide was removed from factories. I said it might be converted into sulphuric acid by reacting it with water. He then asked me what happened to the sulphuric acid. I finally came up with the idea that it was neutralised with a base and I then mentioned a few bases until I came up with calcium carbonate which is generally used in industry because it is cheap. He seemed very pleased at me getting this.

I then asked a question on sponsorship. After answering this he asked if I had any more questions, to which I said no. He then told me that there were still 10 minutes left and proceeded to ask me how Britain had managed to reduce its emissions of carbon dioxide. After some thought I told him I didn't know. He told *me it was due to the conversion of coal power stations to natural gas fueled power stations. I then realised it was because coal contains longer carbon chains, which produce more carbon dioxide when burned, which was correct.*

I again thought that this interview went well. I was very relieved that he didn't ask me any detailed questions on my subjects as I hadn't really studied them enough.

On the 4 January I got an offer - AAA.

Exercise 8

Make your own critical comments on this interview. We suggest you use the same style as in Case Study 1. Compare with our comments that follow.

Comments on Exercise 8

1. The student has a good start by getting an opportunity to discuss the New Scientist article that he had prepared beforehand and was relevant to Chemical Engineering. Note that the 'informal chat' had more technical content than expected.

2. The candidate had prepared for questions on his school project, and showed initiative in researching areas outside of schoolwork. Leaving his sample of Viscose behind is not a mistake that will have bearing on the interview beyond damaging confidence.

3. Speaking in terms 'only half understood' is likely to come across as exactly that, and is a poor gamble as the interviewer may well ask for definitions of terms used.

4. The candidate does well in applying simple concepts learned at school, such as solubility and neutralisation, to a practical context, something that is particularly important in engineering. Also original thinking beyond preconceived ideas is in evidence, which is highly prized.

5. In answer to why Britain's carbon dioxide output had dropped, the candidate correctly admitted ignorance, but would have done better by venturing an hypothesis such as 'perhaps because of the decline in manufacturing industry'.

6. The answer to why moving from coal to gas-fired power stations reduces carbon dioxide output is partially correct, and the candidate has shown ability to think on his feet. A full answer would explain that the number of hydrogen atoms per carbon atom is greater in natural gas than coal - this is partly but not exclusively related to chain length.

Sample questions

Below we list by subject some examples of questions that have been asked at Oxford or Cambridge interviews over recent years. This list is certainly not meant to be comprehensive (or representative of the standard of questions in any subject) and the intention is not to enable you to guess questions you might be asked. What it is intended to do is give a flavour of the style and variety of question used. What should be obvious is the extraordinary range both of subject matter and of style of questioning - some questions seem straightforward school bookwork, others will bear no relation to anything you are familiar with; some can be answered in two minutes, others could take up the whole interview. This realisation is key to understanding the Oxbridge interview: it is entirely futile to attempt to 'know' the answers to everything you could be asked. You must be ready to respond at the time to whatever is thrown at you; the crucial thing is to keep doing your best under difficult circumstances.

Another important point is that no two interviews are the same. Each candidate will be asked different questions and will respond in a different way. There is no linear scale of what is right and what is wrong. Something new is created in each interview; it is not unknown for the interviewers to learn something themselves. The point here is that there is no simple direct comparison between candidates in different interviews. Some will be asked extremely difficult questions, others quite straightforward ones - neither is necessarily an advantage. The aim is to display flair and ability, not to produce some correct answers. Bear these points in mind when scanning the following list of questions.

Looking at questions in subjects other than your own will be worthwhile too, since you are primarily interested in style rather than content. You will notice that for some subjects, rather few questions are given; this is largely a consequence of the nature of the subject. In English, for example, much of an interview will centre on what you have read, comparing it to other texts and putting it in context. In languages, discussion of texts given during the interview - or distributed just before - is very common; similarly in philosophy. It is rather hard to give sample questions for this type of interview, since it is much more of an evolving dialogue than a question and answer session. Do your best to envisage how such a discussion might develop for a passage you have read recently. Questions that may appear easy may lead onto an extensive discussion. Some of the very specific questions listed (on the works of Descartes, Virgil or Jane Austen) will refer to interests expressed by the candidates or books they have read. If possible, try using these questions for practice interview situations.

Archaeology and Anthropology
How has consciousness evolved?

Consider both biological and social arguments for incest taboos.

Give a cultural analysis for Princess Diana's funeral.

How has the use of space in houses changed over history?

What are the key points in Dawkin's "The Selfish Gene"?

What is the role of myth?

Architecture
Tell me about your drawings - what medium do you like best?

Are there any periods or architects that particularly interest you?

Do you know any architects?

Art history
What are the relationships between perception and creativity, and between vision and photography?

What galleries or exhibitions have you visited recently?

Discuss the paintings on the walls of my room.

Biochemistry

Write down the equation for aerobic respiration. What happens in the absence of oxygen?

How do signals travel along nerves?

Biological Sciences
What is a mitochondrion? Why do you only inherit mitochondrial genes from your mother?

Why don't animals have wheels?

What was Lamarck's contribution to the development of the theory of natural selection?

Why do leaves have their stomata on the lower surface?

What are the causes of Down's Syndrome?

Discuss ways in which plants are adapted to dry conditions.

Why are big, fierce animals so rare?

Chemistry
Explain the bonding in benzene.
"Proteins as catalysts". Discuss.

Write down an organic reaction you have studied at school and explain its mechanism.

What do you understand by the term "activation energy"? Has it any relation to enthalpy of reaction?

Why does the boiling point of water rise as salt is dissolved in it?

Classics

What have you read from Horace?

How was Virgil influenced by Homer? How do they differ?

Read and comment on this passage from Herodotus?

"Swayed by the Spartan's oratory, and fearing for their fruit, they decided to revolt from Athens" - has diplomacy changed since Thucydides?

Computer Science

What parts make up a computer?

Every two years the size of computers halves and their speed doubles - can this continue?

Can machines think?

Write down a list of prime numbers. Highlight those of the form $n^2 - 1$. Explain.

Economics

Discuss perfect and imperfect competition.

Compare Keynesian and classical macroeconomics.

What was new about the ideas of Milton Friedman?

Should the reduction of inflation be a major goal of government policy?

What are the origins of wage inflation?

What are the effects of currency speculation?

Are large or small companies more successful?

Should governments subsidise agriculture?

Engineering

What is the Cartesian equation for a circle? Sketch the graph of $x^2+2x+y^2 = 0$.

Give the next two numbers in the following sequence: 0,1,1,2,3,5.

Use momentum to explain how an aerofoil works.

Consider the forces when pushing a ten-kilogram block along a metal plate.

If a lorry carrying a cargo of birds passed over a bridge but was just ten kilograms too heavy, could the driver overcome this obstacle by beating the side of his lorry with a stick?

A closed box with no external forces acting on it is sitting on a frictionless surface. If people were running around inside the box, could the box move along the surface?

A ruler is held up by two fingers, one at an end and one between the other end and the centre. What happens as the fingers are brought together?

What can you tell me about elasticity?

Plot graphs of stress against strain for steel and concrete.

Explain the purpose and design of a flying buttress.

English

What do you read in your spare time?

Where does your love of literature stem from?

The writing of Sylvia Plath has been described as

"an assault on the ears of an uninterested audience". What do you think?

How does art relate to English Literature?

Geography
Is it fair to say that Geography is what Geographers do?

What evidence is there for human influences on climate? What problems are there in predicting climate?

What theories describe the distribution of population on an isotropic plain? What limitations are there to their generality?

What advantages are there for retailers to concentrate their activities in malls rather than disperse throughout towns? Should this be encouraged?

Geology
Sketch the structure of the earth.

What causes volcanoes?

What methods can we use to date samples of rock or sediment. What sources of error are there?

History
What was the religious policy of Phillip II?

Was John Locke a rationalist?

Is national character a useful concept in History?

Do you think that the concept of nationalism useful in considering European History before the eighteenth century?

Should archaeologists and historians talk more to each other?

When was the English monarchy at its strongest?

How long do you think the current capitalist system will last?

Law

(Almost always you will be asked to read a set passage immediately before law interviews - often insufficient time is given).

What have you read in the papers recently which relates to international law?

What do you know about employment legislation?

To what extent do you think that people who want to get married should be left to settle their rights and obligations to each other?

What is the difference between intention and foresight?

Maths

Each room in a house has an even number of doors leading out of it. Prove that the exterior of the house has an even number of doors. [Hint - consider equipping the house with door handles].

If we take three sticks of random length, what is the probability that they can form (a) a triangle, (b) a triangle with no internal angle greater than ninety degrees? [Hint - is there a geometric analogy for the solution?]

If there are three towns linked by two roads each of which has a probability p of being blocked by snow, what is the probability of getting from the first to the third town? If a road is built from the first to the third town with the same probability of being blocked, what is the new probability of getting from the first to the third town? [Hint - consider the probability of not getting from the first to third town.]

Consider digging a tunnel through the centre of the earth, to the other side. Describe the motion of a body dropped into this tunnel.

Medicine

How might gene therapy be used in treating cystic fibrosis?

What is amniocentesis?

How would you design a brain?

What would life be like without enzymes?

What is unusual in the way prions cause disease?

What is the most important medical advance in the last three decades?

What ethical issues are involved in the use of foetal tissue in treatment?

What is current government policy on health and medicine?

There are four patients in end-stage kidney failure:
(i) a 26 year old single mother with three children
(ii) a 49 year old woman who cares for her elderly

mother who has been paralysed since having a stroke two years ago
(iii) an 18 year old male history student
(iv) a 22 year old male who has severe learning difficulties.
There is one kidney available for transplantation and one dialysis machine. Which patient do you decide to transplant and who do you put on dialysis?

Modern and Medieval Languages
(Grammar, comprehension, reading and translation tests are very common, during or before interviews).

What did you find interesting about The Picture of Dorian Gray?

What do you consider the importance of Welsh verse forms to G.M. Hopkins?

What insights into Russian culture does 'The Government Inspector' give us?

What is decadence?

What are the main influences of Russia on mainland Europe?

Read and translate this passage from Madame Bovary.

Tell me about Brecht? Define Marxism.

Music
(Harmonising, keyboard and aural tests are common.)

Consider Bach as a religious composer.

Which areas of music interest you and why?

How did Wagner's operas influence the history of Western music?

Oriental Studies
Alexander the Great - how could one man come to control such a vast area?

Do you think an hour a week justifies doing Japanese at degree level?

Do you know much about Japanese culture?

Tell me a bit about Zen Buddhism.

What are the problems of the modern Middle East?

Is there an East/West divide?

Philosophy
Analyse the discussion provided between two fictional characters.

Great leaps in thinking are often made almost simultaneously by independent people - what do you think?

Can faith in quantum physics and invisible forces tie in with faith in an invisible god?

Discuss Plato's theory of knowledge.

How would you define consciousness?

Discuss Heidegger's "Concept of Time"

Physics
Why is it not strictly true to say that one planet

orbits another?

Explain how we know a centripetal force exists and how we can prove the presence of this force?

Why is the sky blue?

How would using a square wave differ from a sinusoidal wave when applying both to a transformer?

What is the equation for the motion of a pendulum? What approximation must be made?

Derive the equation for the discharge of a capacitor.

Draw graphs of current, voltage and charge on a capacitor against time for a capacitor discharging through a resistor.

Psychology

Comment on the reliability of IQ scores.

To what extent should we trust our introspection?

Define the concept of statistical significance. Are prior expectations of a test's result important?

Social and Political Sciences

What is the future of socialism?

What do you think British society will be like in twenty-five years time?

How does the British political landscape differ now from what it was in 1983?

Is there a tension between British nationalism and local patriotism?

Does the welfare state trap people in poverty?

Will the Kyoto summit have any real consequences?

Discuss criminal responsibility with reference to war crimes, recent cases and youth crimes.

Does the response to the death of Princess Diana represent media hype or a genuine recognition of grief?

Theology

What is meant by "existentialism"?

What is meant by "self" in Buddhism?

What do you think of the books you have read by D.H. Lawrence?

What did Kant have to say about proving God's existence?

CONCLUSION

There is no magic formula for getting into Oxbridge. Success requires talent, hard work and a healthy dollop of good fortune. No amount of preparation can guarantee you a place. To achieve this you will need to have, and, just as importantly, be capable of displaying under the rather odd circumstances of the Oxbridge entry system, a high level of intellectual ability. Do not let this be exaggerated, though, by the Oxbridge mystique. You need to be interested and good at your chosen subject, but it is certainly not necessary to be the next Bertrand Russell, so why not have a go?

It is, however, very easy to destroy your chances of getting in to Oxbridge by failing to prepare properly for the quirky admissions process. One of our principal aims in writing this book was to give you a good insight into what preparations are necessary and how to carry them out most efficiently. This has been achieved partially by the text, but just as importantly by the use of the exercises that we have set for you. Writing down your ideas in this organised manner will ensure that your thoughts are ordered, coherent and relevant, and also will help to embed them in your mind for recall under the pressure of interview. They will, in addition, be readily available for reassurance prior to interviews or tests. Much of the detail of preparation is of course subject-specific; we believe, however, that our structure is generally applicable. It is always sad to see candidates fail simply because they have been unable to display their talents, personality and ability in the short space of time available to them. We know that this is often caused by an ignorance (quite understandable) of the process and what is required to succeed in it. Following this guide will maximise your chances of demonstrating your true worth.

Any selection process inevitably involves a significant random element and the more competitive the process, the more true this is. Oxbridge entry is highly competitive and chance is inevitably going to be important. Each interviewer will usually see several dozen candidates; time is limited and exhaustion, irritation and prejudice cannot be legislated against. Oxford and Cambridge are very diverse and decentralised institutions; much of their academic and social strength stems from this. The admissions system is no exception; it is carried out, autonomously, by around thirty colleges in each university and each of these colleges further subdivides for the many subjects they cater for. Each year several hundred academics are involved in admissions. Candidates' failure to successfully negotiate this complex system only adds to the random element in the admissions system.

The second major aim of this book is to help you to understand how the system operates. This will aid you in making informed choices to optimise your tactical advantages and to aid you in getting what you want from the system. We aim to put you in a position to make rational decisions rather than hopeful guesses in your application.

Levels of preparation for Oxbridge admissions vary enormously. In our experience most candidates are remarkably poorly prepared. This only enhances the advantage to those who know what to expect and how to deal with it. This situation is a considerable hindrance to the fair and open access which both Oxford and Cambridge aspire to. It is our hope that this book will go some way to redressing this. We have laid out clearly authoritative and practical information and wish to make this equally available to all candidates. Mystique has no place in an equitable admissions process and we have done what we can to lay the system bare.

This book will not get you a place at Oxbridge. Only you can do that. It should help you to maximise your chances and display yourself at your best. We hope it will also encourage you to apply and make the process more enjoyable and less traumatic.

Good luck!

APPENDIX I

INFORMATION SOURCES

Oxford University Prospectus
Oxford Colleges Admissions Office
University Offices
Wellington Square
Oxford OX1 2JD
Telephone: (01865) 270207 or 27021
Fax: (01865) 270708
Web site address: http://www.ox.ac.uk

Oxford Written Tests
Samples of written tests for most subjects can be requested from the Oxford Colleges Admissions Office

The Oxford University Alternative Prospectus
Oxford University Student Union
New Barnet House
28 Little Clarendon Street
Oxford OX1 2HU
Telephone: (01865) 270777
Fax: (01865) 270778

Cambridge University Prospectus
Cambridge Intercollegiate Applications Office
Administrative Secretary
Kellet Lodge,
Tennis Court Road
Cambridge CB2 1QJ
Telephone: (01223) 333308
Fax: (01223) 366383
Web site address: http://www.cam.ac.uk

The Cambridge University Alternative Prospectus
The Cambridge University Students' Union
11-12 Trumpington Street
Cambridge CB2 1QA
Telephone: (01223) 333313
Fax: (01223) 323244

STEP Papers
Publications Department
University of Cambridge Local Examinations Syndicate
1 Hills Road
Cambridge CB1 2EU

Cambridge University Guide to Courses
Cambridge University Press Bookshop
1 Trinity Street
Cambridge
CB2 1SZ
Telephone: (01223) 333333

Ordering Further Copies

To order please forward £9.95 plus £1.00 p&p per copy to:

Vine House Distribution Ltd.,
Waldenbury, North Common,
Chailey, East Sussex,
BN8 4DR.
Tel: (01825) 723398   Fax: (01825) 724188.

Credit card orders for Visa and Access may be placed by telephone or Fax. Orders may also be placed by cheque, P.O., or using a Purchase Order form from your school.

Please send me a copy of "How to get into Oxford and Cambridge: Beating the Boffins". I enclose my cheque or P.O. made payable to Vine House Distribution Ltd for

£ ....

or

Please debit my Access/Visa account for

£ ....

Card Number ....

Expiry Date ....

Signature ....

Date ....

Name ....

Address ....

....

....Post Code ....

Ordering Further Copies

To order please forward £9.95 plus £1.00 p&p per copy to:

Vine House Distribution Ltd.,
Waldenbury, North Common,
Chailey, East Sussex,
BN8 4DR.
Tel: (01825) 723398   Fax: (01825) 724188.

Credit card orders for Visa and Access may be placed by telephone or Fax. Orders may also be placed by cheque, P.O., or using a Purchase Order form from your school.

Please send me a copy of "How to get into Oxford and Cambridge: Beating the Boffins". I enclose my cheque or P.O. made payable to Vine House Distribution Ltd for

£ ....

  or

Please debit my Access/Visa account for

£ ....

Card Number ....

Expiry Date..

Signature ....

Date...

Name ....

Address ....

....

....Post Code ....